A Pilgrim's Guide to
LOURDES

and the surrounding area

David Houseley and Peter Latham

Editorial and Revisions – Andrew Houseley

Pilgrim Book Services Limited

© Pilgrim Book Services Limited and David Houseley 2010
ISBN 978-0-9532511-7-9

Published by Pilgrim Book Services Ltd., P.O. Box 27, Woodbridge, Suffolk, England IP13 9AU

 www.pilgrimbooks.com

Second Edition
First Edition pubd. by Egon Publishers, 1991 – as The Pilgrim's Guide to Lourdes by David Houseley and Peter Latham.

Designed by Bob Vickers
Cover designs by Fielding Design
Maps by Rodney Paull
Photographs © Durand, Lourdes, and © Andrew Houseley
Printed in Great Britain by Belmont Press

MIX
Paper from
responsible sources
FSC
www.fsc.org
FSC® C015185

Adapted from the original text (1991) with much gratitude to David Houseley and the late Fr. Peter Latham, past Pilgrimage Director of the Society of Our Lady of Lourdes.

The publishers are grateful for the assistance of The Sanctuaires Notre-Dame de Lourdes and The Archdiocese of Glasgow.

Every effort has been made to contact holders of material which appears in this book. The publishers and author apologise for any errors and omissions. The Mass © International Committee on English in the Liturgy, Inc. 'Holy Virgin, by God's decree' © Kevin Mayhew Limited

Cover picture: The Grotto Massabielle at night – Br. Lawrence Lew O.P.

CONTENTS

Part 1
WHY PILGRIMAGE?

All religions have places whose connection with certain persons or events make them special to the adherents of the faith – eg Jerusalem is a city above all others held holy because of Abraham, Jesus and Mohammed, each of whom knew the place, so it is a shrine for Jews, Christians and Moslems. The believers of these faiths want to tread the same ground the holy person trod – and so they visit the shrine, they make a pilgrimage.

So a pilgrimage is a visit to a place held in respect or veneration, where a holy person lives or worked, or an event took place. In the Christian tradition, places associated with Jesus and the Apostles have been places of pilgrimage since the time of the infant church. Sometimes a person was directed to make a pilgrimage, to pray at the shrine of a saint, to express sorrow or repentance for a serious wrong committed (a sin) to another person or to the community of believers.

So there are places of pilgrimage around the world – some are international, like Jerusalem or Rome, some are more local, like Walsingham or Lough Derg.

Before the days of modern travel by rail or sea, and especially by air, to undertake a pilgrimage was a lengthy business, itself requiring much hardship and deprivation – a journey full of hazard, as well as faith. Since the industrial revolution, travelling has become much more commonplace, so that the sense of extreme hardship has been mostly lost. Perhaps with that, so has the meaning of Pilgrimage been altered somewhat, for to visit anywhere in the world now can be done in a matter of days, rather than months or years, so we do not experience the hardship or reparation for sin in the journey itself as the pilgrim had in earlier times.

There is still, however, the experience of being in a place where previously some person lived or died or some event of religious significance happened. People go on pilgrimage to experience something of that momentous person or event.

For the pilgrim of today it may be that a deeper faith is sought rather than the sense of actually arriving at the shrine. For those of no faith it may be that curiosity persuades them to seek to experience something of the faith they see in others.

In the more recent past, shrines have come into being because Mary the Mother of Jesus has delivered a message to mankind by the extraordinary

Bernadette Soubirous, as viewed in the Lourdes Museum

means of appearing to someone – usually of tender years. Lourdes is such a place, where in 1858, 'the Lady' appeared to Bernadette Mary Bernard Soubirous.

The story of these apparitions to a peasant girl so caught the imagination of an age of significant scientific discovery and advancement, that Lourdes was soon established as a major shrine in France, and within decades as a place of international fame and interest.

There must be some interaction between the influences at work in the nineteenth century to account for this. The advances of industry, science, easier travel, were perhaps sowing the seeds of secularisation that have overtaken our own century. The apparitions at Lourdes were a reminder of the claims of a different level of life, or faith, that mankind should not lightly push aside.

So what is a pilgrimage today? It is a journey of faith, much more than a visit to a shrine. The whole of life is seen by believers as being a journey and in a visit to a shrine, some greater meaning, some greater strength, a greater consolation, is sought from the Almighty.

A visit to Lourdes by a sick person is not necessarily, in fact is seldom, a request for the obvious miracle of a cure. It is more usually a request for the gift of patience to be able to deal with the illness, with the rider that if it be God's wish to effect a cure, so be it. It is just as important that one's faith is deepened and strengthened, as it is for a person to be cured in a more natural way. God can and does give a 'miracle' cure on occasions and always answers a prayer of faith. So a visit to a shrine would help us make a better prayer of faith by acknowledging our weaknesses, spiritual and physical, asking for healing (forgiveness and cure), and accepting the will of the Almighty with thanksgiving and praise.

Part 2
THE LOURDES STORY

On 7th January 1844, there was born at the Boly Mill in Lourdes, a girl child to Francois and Louise Soubirous, a poor family of millers.

She was named Bernadette and was the first of four children. The family had a difficult time trying to survive the numerous vicissitudes of life. These included an accident in which her mother was burned when she was but a few months old and she was sent to the home of a foster mother, Marie Lagües at the village of Bartrés. Marie had lost her own firstborn and was able to suckle the baby and return her to her natural mother after 18 months, though she was never to be a strong and healthy child.

When she was 10, hard times hit the family and they had to seek cheaper accommodation. Francois became a labourer, finding work wherever he could and Bernadette looked after the younger children whilst her mother found domestic and farm work.

In 1855 a cholera epidemic broke out in Lourdes which left Bernadette in permanent ill health as an asthma sufferer. Francois was able to buy another mill with the money left by Louise's mother, but he was no businessman and within a year became bankrupt. The family soon moved to the Cachot, part of an old gaol, described as a 'foul and sombre hovel' with one tiny room in which 6 people had to live, feed and sleep. After a few months, Bernadette was sent again to Bartrés to work as a maid and shepherdess. To complete the family misery, Francois had been falsely imprisoned for theft and their fortunes had never been at a lower ebb. Whilst at Bartrés, Bernadette began to learn the catechism in preparation for her first communion. She had a rosary, which her younger sister had bought for her, and could recite it, though she had no formal schooling, but the first glimmer of a religious faith had begun to come to her.

Bernadette returned to her family in Lourdes in January of 1858. She was now past her 14th birthday and helped to run the home, such as it was. On the morning of 11th February she discovered that there was no wood for the fire and set out with her sister Toinette-Marie and a friend Jeanne Abadie, to collect some. They came eventually to the grotto known as Massabielle by the river Gave. Carved out of the rock face and washed by a mill stream which came between it and the river, the grotto was a favourite haunt for childrens' adventures. Her two companions had crossed the stream and were in the grotto but Bernadette was slower and still on the other side of the mill stream when she heard a gust of wind and she saw that it was rustling the bushes at the foot of the grotto. Then there was a gentle light and the appearance of a smile coming through a mist. Gradually there appeared a most beautiful girl, dressed all in white and holding a rosary. The apparition smiled and opened her hands in a gesture of welcome, and made the sign of a cross. Bernadette reached for her rosary and recited it. The vision likewise fingered her rosary beads but did not speak, before she finally disappeared. In spite of her confused state, Bernadette could remember every detail of what she had seen and reported it to her companions who, though they had seen nothing, could see that she had been deeply affected. In spite of her remonstrations, the story was repeated at home and the young girl was ordered not to return to the grotto. She did not do so for three days, though in the meantime repeated her story in church at confession.

On February 14th, a Sunday, Bernadette determined to return to the grotto and obtained the grudging permission of her father. Accompanied by a number of other children – for her story had now got around – she went this time to the cliff above the grotto and descended the steep and slippery path and knelt in prayer at its foot. As she recited the rosary, the vision appeared once more. Bernadette was in a trance and her appearance frightened her friends who ran away and it took a very strong man, owner of a nearby mill, to remove the inert body of this tiny waif.

Over the next two days public interest in the strange phenomena the girl had seen began to grow, though most people were sure she was either lying or having dreams. Some even thought she might be possessed of a devil, but in spite of the abuse hurled at her, Bernadette returned again to the grotto on the 18th. The vision appeared again. Bernadette, at the behest of some women, asked her to write down her name. 'It is not necessary' said the vision and asked – **'will you have the graciousness to come here for fifteen days?'** She spoke in the local patois of the Lourdes area, in what Bernadette later described as a sweet and delicate voice. And her parting words to Bernadette were to prove significant – **'I do not promise to make you happy in this world, but in the next'.**

On each of the next three days, the vision again appeared. Bernadette was accompanied by a number of adults – up to 100 on the 21st, but the vision did not speak and no-one but Bernadette saw her. There followed days of enquiry and inquisition but no-one could shake the girls' story. On the 22nd there was no appearance, but on the 23rd the 'Lady' appeared again in silence. On the following day, followed by a crowd now grown to around 300, the vision, in her 8th apparition, asked Bernadette to kiss the ground as a penitence for sinners.

Thursday 25th February was a day of great significance. People were now arriving at the grotto each day as early as 2AM to get a good view as the penitent Bernadette approached the grotto on her knees and kissed the ground in accordance with the previous day's instruction. **'Go drink at the spring and wash yourself in it'** said the apparition. Bernadette was puzzled as she saw no spring, but she scraped away at the soil where the 'Lady' was pointing and found a little muddy water. Later in the day some people returned to the scene and found the small trickle of muddy water had grown in size. As they scraped away at the source, the water became clearer and developed into a stream. They drank from it and washed themselves, somehow feeling that there must be a healing quality in such a miraculously discovered source. The same evening Bernadette was interrogated by the Imperial Prosecutor but he found her impossible to break in spite of threats of jail and orders not to return to the grotto. The populace were by this time supporting Bernadette and authority could find no means of stopping her without making itself look stupid. On the 26th she went again to the grotto, with a crowd of several hundred in attendance, but there was no appearance.

On the 27th, the 'Lady' made her 10th appearance and she came again the next day with Bernadette carrying out her penitence on her knees, as she explained, 'for myself and for others'. March 1st saw 15,000 people at the grotto and a considerable police presence needed to control the crowds, which this time included a priest, unaware that the Dean, Peyramale; had forbidden the clergy to go. What he saw greatly impressed him and led to the Church at last beginning to take the matter seriously. The 'Lady' appeared but said nothing. But on this day there occurred the first miracle of Lourdes – a woman heavily pregnant and suffering from a paralysed hand after a fall, dipped her fingers in the water coming from the spring and found them suddenly opening and supple.

The following day, Tuesday 2nd March, the vision made her 13th appearance and this time there was a command – **'Go and tell the Priests that I wish a Chapel to be built and processions to come here'**, a request she repeated the following day. The message was conveyed by Bernadette to Fr Peyramale, who was confused and could not decide whether to take the girl seriously. He played for time, 'You must ask her to state her name' he told Bernadette. The following day there came the 15th appearance – this was the final day of the 15 She had asked Bernadette to come. There was a huge crowd, but they saw nothing except Bernadette go into an ecstasy. But now the crowds were following Bernadette wherever she went, wanting to touch her and offer money and gifts – all of which she firmly rejected. There were stories of miracle cures – of a blind girl who had been embraced by Bernadette and a boy who could not close his mouth. Neither cure was later substantiated.

There the story might well have ended, with public curiosity dying down and life returning to the normal for the Soubirous family. But on the morning of March 25th, Bernadette felt an inexplicable but irrestible urge to return again to the Grotto. The vision appeared, Bernadette again asked her to reveal her identity. **'I am the Immaculate Conception'** came the staggering reply. By now, the Grotto had become a place of pilgrimage. Thousands came every day to pray and many to take the water in the hope of cure for some ailment or other. Bernadette herself had withdrawn from public life in order to protect herself from the frenzy of the crowds, though on April 7th (the Wednesday of Easter week) she again felt drawn to the Grotto and saw the 'Lady' for the 17th time. Now barriers had been set up to prevent access to the Grotto, but each time they were torn down by the crowd, and the authorities were at a loss to know how to cope with the situation. There were many reports of cures; there were constant prayers and devotions, services and processions, and offerings were left at the Grotto. The Church was still being ambivalent, though the Abbé Peyramale was by now convinced and became a great support to Bernadette, but it was not until four years later that the Bishop of Tarbes finally announced that the Virgin had indeed appeared to Bernadette Soubirous.

Bernadette herself took no part in all the activity which now surrounded the Grotto. She said many times that people should not cross the barriers against the wishes of the authorities and she made it plain that she had never said that cures would take place in Lourdes. There was, however, one final appearance, on July 16th, for which Bernadette, heavily disguised, stayed on the opposite bank of the river. She somehow knew that this was to be the final time, and she described the apparition in glowing terms – 'Never did I see her as beautiful'. She prayed for sinners and for repentance, and did penance, as the 'lady' had asked, setting the precedent for what today remains the central theme of a Pilgrimage to Lourdes.

Bernadette was cross examined by Bishops, by journalists and by an Episcopal Commission. She remained unmoved and unshaken and gradually the story gained credence among the nobility and the hierarchy as it had from the beginning with the ordinary people. Even the Emperor Napoleon III became involved and it was he who finally ordered the removal of all the barriers from the Grotto. The family were moved, at the behest of the Church, to more salubrious accommodation, whilst Bernadette herself was living at the hospice kept by the Sisters of Nevers. She left Lourdes in 1866 to go as a Novice to the convent at Nevers in central France with a view to becoming a nun. Part of her job was that of tending to the sick, but her own health was deteriorating and she died on 16th April 1879 at the age of 35. In 1909 her body was exhumed and found to be incorrupt, and finally in 1933 she became Saint Bernadette, by order of Pope Pius XI.

By that time, of course, Lourdes had become one of the great centres of Pilgrimage. The story of Bernadette Soubirous had become known the world over, and the central themes of prayer, of penance, of forgiveness of sins and the healing of the sick, have remained a compelling reason to make a pilgrimage to this attractive town in the foothills of the Pyrenees.

PRINCIPAL EVENTS IN THE LIFE OF BERNADETTE SOUBIROUS

1844	7th January	She was born at the Boly Mill
	9th January	Baptised at the Parish Church
	November	Taken to her foster mother at Bartrés
1846	April	Returned to her family at Lourdes
1854		Family moves to a cheaper mill
1855		Cholera epidemic leaves Bernadette with chronic asthma. Family leave Lourdes and go to Arcizac.
1856		Famine – Francois Soubirous now bankrupt
1857		Family unable to pay rent and move to Cachot
	November	Bernadette is sent as a maid to the farm at Bartrés
1858	January	She returns to Lourdes
	11th February	The first Apparition
	3rd June	Her first communion
1860	16th July	The 18th and final Apparition
1866		She becomes a boarder at the Hospice
1879	16th April	She goes to Nevers as a Novîce
		Bernadette dies at Nevers, aged 35
1909	22nd September	Her body exhumed and found to be incorrupt
1933	8th December	Bernadette is canonised by Pope Pius XI

The world comes to greet Pope Benedict XVI

The Torchlight Procession

Part 3
A POTTED HISTORICAL BACKGROUND OF LOURDES AND THE PYRENEES

Human remains have been found in the Roussillon which are among the earliest known examples of man in Europe – going back almost 500,000 years – but cave paintings to be seen in various places in the Pyrenees show that life here existed at least 10,000 years BC and there are burial chambers going back to 5,000 BC pointing to continuous occupation from the time.

Celts, Greeks, Romans and Vandals have all left their mark. Hanibal crossed the Pyrenees as well as the Alps – in 214 BC, but history really begins with the Moorish occupation of Spain in the 8th Century AD. They were pushed back over the Pyrenees by Charlemagne (764–814) but not before he had met some severe setbacks, including the famous massacre at Roncesvalles in 778 when his army was returning from the sacking of Pamplona. The Moors were finally driven from the area after the Battle of Las Navas de Tolosa in 1212 by forces from several Christian kingdoms. This was the real beginning of Christianity in the area and it is marked by a number of monastic settlements and romanseque churches still to be seen. However, the area was divided between various feudal monarchs, who were forever fighting among themselves for territory and the large number of fortified churches and villages (bastides) you can see today are reminders of this era.

Through a series of convenient marriages, power shifted to the English King Henry II, who controlled a large part of France from Calais to the Pyrenees. His son, Richard the Lionheart went this way to the Crusades, but the Spanish also launched numerous forays across the mountains in efforts, sometimes successful, to gain control, and the French were always looking for something to take in exchange. These campaigns had largely fizzled out by the beginning of the 13th century and the Treaty of Corbeil (1258) saw France and Spain agreeing to respect each other's territory. English claims to the throne of France had set off the Hundred Years War in 1338 and bit by bit the English rule was chipped away.

The Centre of Pilgrimage

The accession to the throne in 1589 of Henri IV, first Protestant King of France, who was born in Pau, brought a period of freedom of religion to the area. The south was largely Protestant but Henri became a Catholic, to enable him to assimilate Paris and the north, and decreed that all could choose which religion to follow. This only lasted until the suppression of the Protestant strongholds by Cardinal Richelieu after the death of Henri in 1610. By 1635, France and Spain were again at war, but this ended with the signing of the Treaty of the Pyrenees at Hendaye in 1659. Two years later, the most convenient of all marriages took place in nearby St Jean de Luz –that between the 'Sun King' Louis XIV and Maria Teresa, the Infanta of Spain.

Napoleon launched his take over of Spain in 1808, soon after becoming Emperor of France, thus starting the Peninsular War, and incidentally re-popularising some of the Roman spa towns of the Pyrenees as hospital bases for his troops. His undoing was at the hand of Wellington, whose English army chased him across the mountains and many of whose officers took a fancy to such towns as Pau and Bagnères. They founded a considerable English colony in those places, some signs of which are still evident.

The period of Bernadette's life was a turbulent one for France, which was a monarchy at the time she was born, with Louis-Philippe as King, but became a Republic in 1848, when she was four years old. The Second Empire was proclaimed in 1852, under Louis Napoleon (he it was who became involved in the controversy surrounding the visions at the Grotto of Massabielle); but the nation reverted to republicanism in 1870 after the defeat of Napoleon III by the Prussians. Thus Bernadette was born into a country which during her lifetime was twice a monarchy and twice a republic, though these matters of state would hardly have touched life at the level it was lived by ordinary people such as the Soubirous family.

The Spanish Civil War (1936–39) saw a great deal of action on the Spanish side of the mountains and a huge influx of refugees crossing into France. This was to be followed a year or two later by refugee traffic in the opposite direction; Frenchmen fleeing from Nazi occupation to join General de Gaulle's Free French forces in London, and then escape routes for Jews, escaping Allied Prisoners of War and shot down airmen, who made use of a highly organised escape organisation set up by the French Resistance which produced a large number of local heroes and martyrs.

Thus the Pyrenees have over the centuries been anything but the natural barrier they would seem to be. Perhaps it is the natural desire of man to conquer anything which seems to be in the way – 'just because it is there' – which has made so many want to cross them, and certainly that would apply to the high tradition of exploration and mountaineering which has produced its own set of heroic figures who are remembered in a number of local museums. History and geography have combined to make the Pyrenean people a very independent and highly resourceful race.

The Castle at Pau

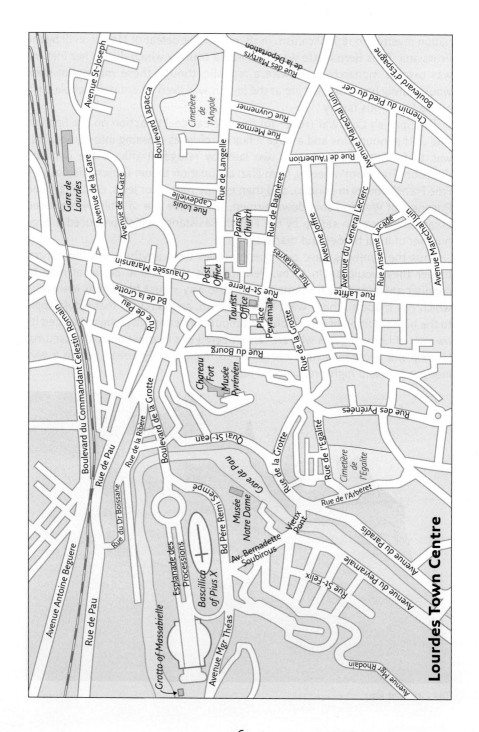

Lourdes Town Centre

Part 4
LOURDES –
THE DOMAINE

The Domaine is that area, spreading on both sides of the River, which contains all of the Sanctuaries. It is controlled by the Church and has two main entrances, approached from the Old Bridge (Vieux Pont) and Ave Bernadette Soubirous, which leads up to St Joseph's Gate, or from the Pont St Michel which brings one immediately to St Michael's Gate.

The lower part of the town, in which the Domaine is situated, is where the majority of hotels for pilgrims are – indeed it seems to contain nothing but hotels, cafes and a very large number of souvenir shops. Much of what is sold in these establishments is in rather poor taste – it is possible to find quality, but only with difficulty.

A preliminary visit to find your way around the Domaine is strongly advised, before you set out to take part in any Masses or processions, and you will

The Basilicas from the Gave de Pau

probably want to do this on the evening of your first arrival. If you can be there during the Torchlight Procession (from about 8.30PM), it will greatly enhance your first impressions.

If we enter first by **ST JOSEPH'S GATE**, we see a statue of the husband of Our Lady upon the left hand gate post holding the infant Jesus. Inside, also on the left is a group in white stone showing the healing of the sick. These are examples of the many items of statuary within the Domaine – indeed there is something of an embarrassment of riches and a store has had to be established for those surplus to requirements. Most have been given over the years by national or regional Pilgrimages to Lourdes.

There are information kiosks in this area also, and on the right notices give the programme of Masses for the day, showing in what language each is to be conducted. There are always several Masses in English to select from and they are rotated around the major shrines so each language group has the chance to celebrate at all of them. To the right is a building called the Permanances,

St Joseph's Gate

which contains the temporary offices of each official pilgrimage currently in town. If you are with one of these, this is where your enquiries may be made. Just beyond this building is the only commercial area within the Domaine. It has the main information centre, telephones and a bookshop (librarie), which also sells CDs, DVDs and videos. A Post Office might be a useful addition. There are wisely no refreshment facilities within the Domaine but many just outside the gates. Here also are the offices of much of the administration and of the Medical Bureau, of which more later. We are led within a few yards to the broad open space with the great Rosary Square fronting the Basilicas to our left, whilst on our right the wide avenue known as the Esplanade leads to St Michael's Gate.

Between the two, however, is an important focal point – the statue of **THE CROWNED VIRGIN**. She was 'crowned' in 1876 and stands in the centre of a bed of roses, surrounded by railings which are usually bedecked with bouquets of many more roses placed there by pilgrims in adoration or thanksgiving. This is the place to meet, the centrepoint of the Domaine. But before we proceed further, let us enter instead from **ST MICHAEL'S GATE**.

Just inside this gate we are faced with a statue known as the Breton Calvary, because it was presented by the people of Brittany. On the gateposts themselves are statues of the Archangels Gabriel (on the right) and Raphael – the companion of travellers.

To the left is the first of several entrances to the vast underground **BASILICA OF ST PIUS X**. Familiarly known as SPD and once described unflatteringly as having an interior rather like the inside of a whale, the Basilica was completed in 1958 to cope with the centenary celebrations of Lourdes and was consecrated by Cardinal Roncalli, who became Pope John XXIII a few months later. It can take 25,000 or more people, but at least 5,000 seated. Its main purpose in the weekly programmes is to hold the International Masses held every Sunday and Wednesday, and on Feast days. The sight and sound of this place in the full flood of praise is something to remember. Around the walls are modern paintings on the glass marking the Stations of the Cross and Mysteries of the Rosary. The oval shape of the Basilica – some 200 metres long and 80 wide, together with the concrete ribbed

The Breton Calvary

Archangel Raphael at St Michael's Gate

Inside the Basilica of St Pius X

construction enables everyone to see the celebration at the great central altar. In inclement weather the afternoon procession of the Blessed Sacrament and Blessing of the Sick is held here instead of outside.

Back in the open air and proceeding along the Esplanade towards the Basilicas, we see on our right the entrance to one of the smaller chapels, that of **ST JOSEPH**. Also partially underground, this has a simple but effective interior and though it can seat 450 people it has a feeling of intimacy which many people like. There is a small statue of Our Lady of Walsingham which was given by the Anglican Society of Mary in England. Next to the Chapel is the **ACCUEIL JEAN-PAUL II**, one of the centres dedicated to receiving sick pilgrims during their stay in Lourdes. It also contains the Medical Bureau where claims to have been healed through the intercession of Our Lady of Lourdes are received. Behind this centre and looking across the St Bernadette Footbridge lies the impressive new **ACCUEIL NOTRE DAME**, re-sited from where the Accueil Jean-Paul II now stands. This is one of two main hospitals for accommodating sick and disabled pilgrims and those who accompany them during their stay in Lourdes.

Now we are back to the statue of the Crowned Virgin, and if we stand with our backs to her, we can look ahead to **ROSARY SQUARE**. Here, some thousands of people congregate daily following the two main processions – up to 40,000 have been known. The Basilicas themselves rise in three levels before us. To right and left great ramps enable wheelchairs to be pushed to the

The Domaine

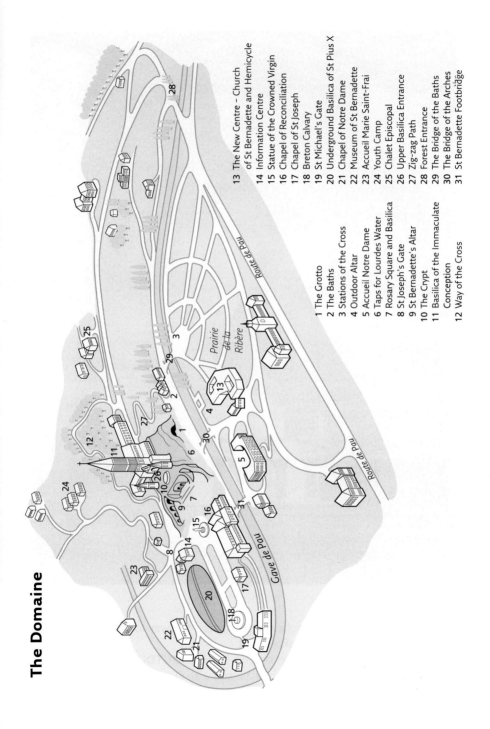

1 The Grotto
2 The Baths
3 Stations of the Cross
4 Outdoor Altar
5 Accueil Notre Dame
6 Taps for Lourdes Water
7 Rosary Square and Basilica
8 St Joseph's Gate
9 St Bernadette's Altar
10 The Crypt
11 Basilica of the Immaculate Conception
12 Way of the Cross
13 The New Centre – Church of St Bernadette and Hemicycle
14 Information Centre
15 Statue of the Crowned Virgin
16 Chapel of Reconciliation
17 Chapel of St Joseph
18 Breton Calvary
19 St Michael's Gate
20 Underground Basilica of St Pius X
21 Chapel of Notre Dame
22 Museum of St Bernadette
23 Accueil Marie Saint-Frai
24 Youth Camp
25 Chalet Episcopal
26 Upper Basilica Entrance
27 Zig-zag Path
28 Forest Entrance
29 The Bridge of the Baths
30 The Bridge of the Arches
31 St Bernadette Footbridge

Prairie de la Ribère

Route de Pau

Route de Pau

Gave de Pau

Altar of St Bernadette

higher ones, and under the arches on the right is the way to the Grotto. But we shall leave that to the climax of our visit.

Before we go inside, we see on the left the **OUTDOOR ALTAR OF ST BERNADETTE**, decorated in fine mosaic and with Our Lady of Guadaloupe and St Paschal Baylon in attendance.

At ground level, the first of the major Churches is the **ROSARY BASILICA** which was consecrated in 1901 and can hold 1,500 people. Built in Byzantine style, in the form of a Greek Cross, it has 15 side chapels dedicated to the mysteries of the Rosary. A large mosaic above the altar bears the inscription 'Par Marie a Jésus' (through Mary to Jesus).

Steps at either side lead to the next level, with statues of St Peter and St Paul at the foot. If we use the ramp instead we shall pass a number of statues of the saints – on the left side those of Remigius, Vincent de Paul, Joachim, Bernard and John the Baptist, whilst on the right hand ramp are St Martin of Tours, St Louis de Montfort, St Anne (holding the baby Mary), St Hyacinth and St John the Apostle. The terrace we have now reached provides an excellent viewpoint, both for the ceremonies and for a general view of the Domaine and further afield – look towards the Chateau over the town. Here also you have a close up view of the dome over the Rosary Basilica, with a huge golden Crown and Cross, given by Irish pilgrims in 1924.

Over the entrance to the **CRYPT**, is a mosaic portrait of Pope Pius X. He is remembered for his encouragement of early communion for young people and just inside is a bronze of him giving the sacrament to a boy and a girl. The Crypt was the first church to be built following the admonition of the Virgin through Bernadette. It is entered by a long corridor, hewn from the solid rock by a gang of 25 men, including Bernadette's father, working day and night. The interior is vaulted with marble decoration. It was consecrated in 1866 and Bernadette was herself present, though hidden from public view. The Crypt is now reserved for silent prayer and adoration.

Outside, it is possible to cross the road through a gate to the Way of the Cross, but we shall return there after climbing some more steps to the **BASILICA OF THE IMMACULATE CONCEPTION**, or Upper Basilica. There is access for wheelchairs from the roadway and the two smaller spires at either side contain lift shafts. The Basilica was consecrated in 1876 and its chancel stands immediately above the Grotto. Over the door is a mosaic portrait of Pope Pius IX, who interestingly had defined the doctrine of the immaculate conception just four years before the Virgin appeared to Bernadette, saying 'I am the Immaculate Conception'. High above is the great spire and the clock which chimes the tune of the Lourdes Hymn. Inside, there are chapels dedicated to St Anne (right side) and St Joan of Arc (left) whilst the most remarkable feature is the amount of stained glass. Windows in each of the 15 side chapels reflect the story of Lourdes from the first apparition up to 1876, whilst the larger ones above recall the mystery of the Immaculate Conception.

If we go outside again and look across the road, we see the entrance to the **WAY OF THE CROSS**, an uphill climb of about a mile. At the first station is a Scala Sancta, a copy of the one in Rome which in turn is said to come originally from the House of Pilate in Jerusalem – and thus the one which Jesus would

The statue of Our Lady

have climbed during his trials. It is customary for pilgrims to climb this on their knees, and many do the whole Via Dolorosa in bare feet. At each Station is a group of life size figures in cast iron and bronze. This is an act of penance for which most people reserve a separate half day from their visits to the Domaine – and in fact the Way of the Cross is strictly speaking outside the property of the Domaine. It can be approached by the road which leads uphill by the side of St Joseph's Gate.

A little way up the road on the right is a gate leading back into the Domaine and a zig-zag path which leads down to the Grotto. This is remarkable for the statue of a blind man kneeling on one knee at the cross. The inscription can be translated as 'It is better to have the eyes of faith opened than to recover those of the body'. The path is a rather easier route down to the Grotto than the steep bank at the same point, down which Bernadette and her companion fell.

But we shall approach the **GROTTO** at ground level, from Rosary Square. As we pass under the arches of the ramp, we see on the left booths for the sale of candles in many different sizes, and taps for Lourdes water. All of these will be spoken of later, but if you wish to buy a candle, do so now and hand it to one of the attendants who will place it on a trolley which will gradually be taken closer to the Grotto itself. A plaque above the taps recalls the admonition given to Bernadette – 'Go drink at the fountain' (Allez boire a la fontaine), and beneath it 'Like Bernadette, wash your face and ask God to cleanse your heart'. Nearby the other messages given to Bernadette by 'the Lady' are written in marble.

You are asked to keep silence in this area as it is of course the centrepiece of your Pilgrimage and the most revered place within the Domaine. Note that the wide promenade area is a comparatively recent addition. In the time of Bernadette the river flowed very close to the Grotto, though there was also a small mill stream which separated her from the Grotto during the apparitions. The river has been diverted to allow more space for Pilgrims and when no ceremony is in progress there are seats for quiet meditation and a queue forms to file past the inner part of the Grotto. In front of the seats are two mosaic plaques set into the paving, one marking the spot at which Bernadette knelt before 'the Lady', and the other shows the course of the Mill Stream, which is no more.

The statue of Our Lady which dominates the Grotto is by Joseph Fabisch and is set at the spot at which she appeared to Bernadette and in her attitude at the moment when she spoke the words 'I am the Immaculate Conception'. These words are inscribed below in the local patois in which she spoke them. The rock below the statue is worn smooth by the touch of so many Pilgrims and there is a tabernacle used during the Masses held here. As you file past you will pass a tin box known as 'Our Lady's Post Box' into which Pilgrims place their messages and petitions on behalf of friends. Take care not to include any money as the contents are regularly burnt. The source of the spring can be seen on the left side of the Grotto, now illuminated and covered with glass. Above hangs a selection of crutches left behind by those who have been cured, but the vast majority had to be cleared away.

Beyond the Grotto are the Baths (see below) and within the woods alongside the river is one of the Cinemas which show films of the life of Bernadette, and this whole area is a delightful place of peace and quiet for contemplation and a quiet stroll.

ACROSS THE RIVER, accessed by two footbridges, is the vast open space known as the Meadow, or Prairie. It has several outdoor altars, including one by the river just across from the Grotto, and a larger one which was used by Pope John Paul II during his visit in 1983. Close to the lower footbridge, is the strikingly designed **TENT OF ADORATION**, where the Blessed Sacrament is exposed from 8AM each day before being taken to the Procession at 5PM. A modern complex, called the **NEW CENTRE**, completed in 1988, includes a large church, that of **ST BERNADETTE** which can take 5,000 people, but is normally divided into two unequal sections. Connected to it is the **HEMICYCLE**, a Lecture Theatre to seat 500, and within the complex there are a number of conference rooms for use by groups of various sizes.

Along a flat walk by the River is a set of **STATIONS OF THE CROSS**, at ground level, which are especially useful for those in wheelchairs who cannot make the hilly Way of the Cross. There are in fact 17 'Stations' here – sculpted in white marble by the Belgian Maria de Faykod – commissioned in 2001 and installed in time for the 150th anniversary of the Apparitions in 2008. Back towards the New Centre is the **WATER WALK**, a riverside path with nine fountains providing another opportunity for taking Lourdes water. This time, however, you are encouraged to wash your face, and each fountain displays a different Bible reference and different title for the Blessed Virgin Mary, so it is possible to visit each fountain as part of a liturgy.

Finally, across the river again and back in Rosary Square, diagonally to the left when facing the Statue of the Crowned Virgin, we see the **CHAPEL OF RECONCILIATION**, where there are some fifty Confessionals and there are Priests on duty to hear Confession in many languages, and always in English – times are given on the noticeboard outside.

THE HOLY WATER OF LOURDES

Just along from the Grotto are **THE BATHS**. Most Pilgrims, whether sick or not, feel that a Pilgrimage to Lourdes is not complete without taking a bath in the water from the Holy Spring which came to life under the fingers of Bernadette.

The spring which came so hesitantly to life in 1858 now gushes forth at a rate of up to 27,000 gallons a day, though it suffers from dry summers like everywhere else. The water is stored in huge reservoirs from which it is fed to the many taps, some for washing and others from which to fill containers, and to the bath house. In this there are 14 baths, divided between men and women, and people queue to be bathed by the attendants. Usually there is a big demand and long queues, especially for women, are common, so it is not possible to spend more than a few moments immersed, sufficient just to make a prayer.

Of the recorded 'miracle cures' which have been authenticated – a lengthy and exhaustive process overseen by the Medical Bureau at Lourdes – there are several which have achieved international fame, including the best known British one, that of Jack Traynor of Liverpool in 1923, the details of which were recorded in his own book. It is thought that the majority of 'cures' which occur nowadays are never reported, indeed less than seventy have been pronounced as miraculous though 5,000 more have satisfied the most stringent medical tests. It is important to realise that these 'cures' may take place in any part of the world, either to those who have visited Lourdes and returned home, or to those who have never been to Lourdes at all, but may have been prayed for by pilgrim friends.

Most pilgrimages, both official ones and the smaller, parish groups, bring some sick people with them, together with the able bodied helpers, nurses and doctors to look after them. In some cases they come to pray for people who are too sick to travel, but in either case the care and welfare of the sick is a central part of any pilgrimage to Lourdes.

Part 5
LOURDES – THE TOWN AND AROUND

1. SITES RELATED TO BERNADETTE

There is a number of places in the town and nearby which are associated with the life of Bernadette and which most Pilgrims will want to see. They are, however, well scattered and not all are well signposted, so it is a good idea either to join a guided group or to take a good map. Some quite steep climbs are involved.

Most of the places to be visited are closed between 12 noon and 2PM. There are usually no entrance fees, but there are boxes for donations at each place for its upkeep. We shall take a route which enables most of the sites to be seen in a gentle walk, but they will not be seen in chronological order.

Starting from the Pont St Michel and facing uphill toward the town, we take a right turn almost immediately into the Rue Bernadette Soubirous. After about 100 metres we come on the left to the first of the sites – **THE BOLY MILL**, birthplace of Bernadette. Named after the owner – the Boly family can be traced back to 1670 with some of its origins in London – the building was situated along one of the many mill streams which threaded through the lower part of the town. Most of them have now disappeared. The Mill is simply furnished with numerous reminders of life at the time of her birth – on 7th January 1844. The kitchen on the ground floor with the simple living quarters adjoins the remaining

The Boly Mill

Sites associated with Bernadette

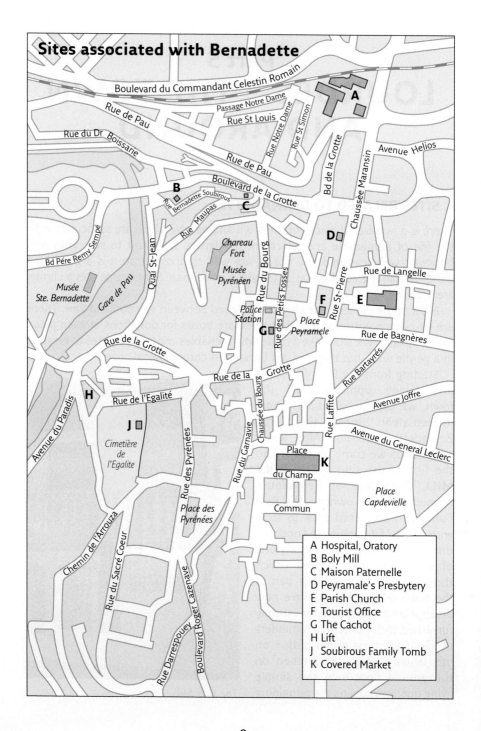

A Hospital, Oratory
B Boly Mill
C Maison Paternelle
D Peyramale's Presbytery
E Parish Church
F Tourist Office
G The Cachot
H Lift
J Soubirous Family Tomb
K Covered Market

mill machinery and workplace. The upper floor has the actual room in which she was born and has some furniture from the time. Bernadette lived the first ten years of her life here, until her father could no longer pay the rent.

Another 100 metres along the same road brings us to Moulin Lacade, or **MAISON PATERNELLE**, so called because it was a mill rented for M. Soubirous after his daughter had become a celebrity and the Church authorities did not want the object of much public attention to appear so poor. The building was comparatively modern – the date 1802 is over the door – and was one of five mills along this street alone. Bernadette never in fact lived here but there are many family photographs and some authentic furniture. Access is by very narrow walkways. There is a small souvenir shop attached.

To reach the **CACHOT**, which is in the Rue des Petits Fosses, is quite a walk, along the Rue du Bourg, turning left at the Police Station and right up the narrow lane onto which the small house directly fronts. This is now a two room property, though the front room was never occupied by the family and is but a place for souvenirs. The tiny rear room, little more than 15 sq. metres, in which lived the parents and four children was but a hovel, already condemned as unfit even for prisoners, for it had been part of the town gaol (cachot = dungeon). It is a place to reflect how low the family had sunk, yet this was the place from which the young girl set out to find firewood, and instead found a vision which has so profoundly affected the whole world.

We are now close to the town centre and can cross the main street to the **PARISH CHURCH**. This was re-built in 1902 so would not have been known to Bernadette, but it contains the font at which she was baptised and a Madonna and Child beside it, which were from the old church. A copy of the entry in the Baptism Register is shown. The large stone cross in front of the building would have been a landmark she recognised as it stood also before the original church. The church crypt contains the tomb of the Abbé Peyramale, who became such an influence on her life.

The Cachot

29

The **PRESBYTERY** of the Abbé Peyramale, which later housed the Public Library, but at the time of writing is closed, is along the main street (turn right coming from the church), standing back from the road in landscaped grounds. This is where Bernadette came to deliver the messages she received from the 'Lady' at the Grotto.

Some way further along this street is the **HOSPICE**, also known as the Oratory. It now stands in the grounds of the modern community hospital at a busy road junction. It has been run by the Sisters of Charity of Nevers – the Order which Bernadette joined – since before her birth, and was then a school. She attended here to prepare for her first communion, eventually becoming a boarder to protect her from the crowds. She stayed until she went to the headquarters of the Order in Nevers in 1866 to become a nun. The old Chapel, in which she made her first communion on 3rd June 1858, can be used by small

The Presbytery of the Abbé Peyramale

groups, but a larger Chapel, which was being built during Bernadette's stay, is also available.

The **SOUBIROUS FAMILY TOMB** in which are interred Bernadette's parents and many of their descendants up to the present time, is in the Cimitère de l'Égalité. Bernadette's own, incorrupt, body is of course in the Chapel at Nevers. The tomb is to the right of the entrance, taking the second path to the left and about 50 metres from the gate. It is of modern grey granite and has little to commend it except for the interest of the family connection and an excellent view to be had across the valley towards the City of the Poor and the Stations of the Cross on the wooded hill beyond.

Close to the cemetery entrance is a lift in which you can ascend or descend to and from the lower town. The bottom station is close to the Pont Vieux.

2. SECULAR SITES AND PAVILIONS

We may be only aware of the spiritual dominance of Lourdes and its story whilst we are here, but the town of Lourdes is physically dominated by three things – the twin peaks of the Pic Béout (790m) and Pic du Jer, and by the Chateau. The two peaks can be distinguished as Pic du Jer has a cross on top.

Unfortunately, the **PIC BÉOUT**, which has a cable car route, is now inaccessible, since the cable car has malfunctioned and nobody has come up with the money to refurbish it. There is a pathway for the hardy, and the reward is an excellent view of the town and beyond to the snow capped Pyrenees. There are also the caves of the Gouffre Béout, some 80 metres deep which were discovered in 1938.

However, the **PIC DU JER**, which is 1,000 metres high, is accessible by a funicular, which starts from the Avenue F Lagardere – some way along the main street from the town centre towards Argelès. At the top is a splendid view and some caves which can be visited without too much effort, as they are not very deep – in fact you emerge higher up the hill.

The **CHATEAU FORT** is important, partly because it contains the Museum of the Pyrenees, but also because of its history. At a time when the town was occupied by the Moors, it was besieged by Charlamagne. The story goes that an eagle caught a large trout from the river but dropped it inside the city walls. The Moorish chief, Mirat, rather than using it to feed his hungry troops, threw it over the walls to trick the French into believing that they had plenty to eat. Mirat was eventually converted to Christianity and took the name Lorus, which has since been corrupted to Lourdes, and so the town is named after him. The town has also adopted the trout as its emblem and it appears in the coat of arms. Well, it's a good story!

The Chateau is reached by a stairway of more than 150 steps from the Place du Fort, or by a lift from close by, or there is a roadway, the Rampe du Fort.

The more recent history of the Chateau includes its ownership by the English crown for two periods during the 13th and 14th centuries. Lord Elgin, the English ambassador to Athens – he of the Marbles – was imprisoned here for a time in 1803 during the Napoleonic wars.

The **MUSEUM OF THE PYRENEES**, which is within the Castle, has examples of crafts, and of furnishings and implements from many periods, and there are some interesting 18th century gilded carvings in the Chapel, mostly brought from the old church in the town. But it is for the history of exploration and mountaineering in the Pyrenees that the Museum is most famous. The primitive equipment used by the early pioneers, the maps and painting of the famous cartographer Franz Schrader, from the late nineteenth century, and numerous tableaux showing the way of life in those times, make this an essential part of one's stay in Lourdes, especially if you are going to explore the mountain areas.

There are several other 'Musées' advertising themselves in the town, but this word generally means an exhibition rather than a museum and most are commercial exploitations. The **Musée de Cire** (87 Rue de la Grotte) has a waxwork tableau of the Lourdes story, The **Musee de Lourdes** (by the Car Park for the Cimetière de l'Égalité) depicts the village at the time of the apparitions, whilst the **Musée de la Nativité** (21 Quai St Jean) presents the early life of Jesus in model form. All these will ask for an entrance fee.

However, there are several displays that do not ask for an entrance fee. One is an art gallery, the **Musée Gemmail** (72 Rue de la Grotte), with modern religious works, including some by a group of artists who work with glass – as in the underground Basilica; but there is also the **Musée Bernadette** (off B'de Pere Rèmi Sempé a few metres from the Domaine) which has a table model of Lourdes in the time of Bernadette which is useful for showing the changed course of the river and streams around the Grotto, important in understanding the story of the Apparitions. There are many artefacts, photographs and mementos of the early days of Pilgrimages. Along the same stretch of road are several other Pavilions which deal with various aspects of Christ's work:- the Missions, the Legion of Mary, Pax Christi, and those for vocational guidance and Christian Unity. Further Pavilions are to be found in the Domaine and the Town, including for handicapped people, and for ways of continuing your Pilgrimage after your return home.

One visit which could usefully be made is to **PETIT LOURDES**, a model village type of display on the edge of town near the Pont Peyramale, not far from the hotel district. This again shows the town as it was in the 1840s and by stripping away the more modern developments enables us to understand the kind of journey the young girl had to make on her excursions to find firewood. It is well done and involves a stroll by the river, ideal for a spare hour or two.

The **CITY OF THE POOR** (Cité Secours St Pierre) is an area consisting of several pavilions for the reception of pilgrims who cannot afford hotel prices. Established originally at the specific request of Bernadette (though on this site only since 1956), the Cité can accommodate over 500 pilgrims, who are allowed to stay for up to five days. Guided tours are arranged and the site can be reached by a long uphill walk from St Joseph's Gate, or there is a bus service from there. Nearby is the **YOUTH CAMP** where more than 3,000 young visitors can be accommodated in dormitories and under canvas.

In Lourdes there are three cinemas which show films of the life of Bernadette. One is within the Domaine, past the Baths, another in the Ave Mgr Schoepfer, opposite St Joseph's Gate and the third the Rue de la Grotte. You will need to refer to the local publicity to find the times of performances in English.

3. FURTHER AFIELD

If you have transport available, or if there are excursions arranged, the following visits are recommended. They are all within a few miles of Lourdes and can easily be enjoyed within half a day.

BARTRÈS, a small village about 4Km from Lourdes (turn left just beyond the hospital, under the railway bridge, following signs to Pau – then immediately right) is where Bernadette spend two periods of her youth. As a baby, when her mother was unable to suckle her, she came to the home of Marie Arravant, from November 1844 until April 1846. She returned there to work as a maid from November 1857 to January 1858. In this latter time, she watched over the sheep, and the thatched barn, or sheepfold (bergerie) is in a field just before the village is reached. An Oratory with a statue of Bernadette at the roadside shows its position. From here, there is a path by which you can walk into the village across the fields, as Bernadette would have done. The farmhouse home of Marie Arravant (sometimes known by her married name of Lagües) has been extensively altered since that time because of a fire but one room has been set aside to show furniture and implements of the time. The Parish Church is worth a visit. It has some wonderful 17th century gilded carvings in the sanctuary showing scenes from the life of St John the Baptist, to whom the church is dedicated. In the churchyard is the grave of Bernadette's foster mother. Some pilgrims like to walk to Bartrès - it is a long uphill climb but there are some good views on the way. Alternatively, a bus service runs from St Joseph's Gate by the Domaine.

THE LAC DE LOURDES is in the same general direction, about 4Km on the main road to Pau (the D940). This is a very pleasant recreational area, with boating and swimming and a picnic area. There is a cafe and a golf course adjoining.

The Way of the Cross at Bétharram

The secondary Pau road, the D937, is the more scenic as it follows the river valley. It goes through the village of **ST PÉ de BIGORRE**, which is worth a stop to see the arcaded main square and a very old church, dating from the 11th century. It was originally part of a Benedictine Abbey, has some interesting old paintings and displays a Key, said to be forged from a link in the chain which held St Peter whilst he was in prison. After 12 Km from Lourdes, you will come to the **GROTTES de BÉTHARRAM**, the largest and most spectacular of the grottoes in the region, with some 5Km of underground galleries which you can traverse by boat and train. The visit takes an hour and a half and commentary is in several languages, including English. The Gave de Pau runs through here and there is a legend that the Virgin Mary saved a young girl from drowning by throwing a branch to her. The nearby village of Bétharram is where Bernedette's sister bought her first Rosary. There is a shrine to St Michael Garricoits, founder of the Order of the Sacred Heart, whose tomb is also there. It is now also a Seminary for Priests wanting to join the Order. The Chapel can be visited and there is an impressive Way of the Cross with Chapels at each Station.

THE PEOPLE WHO MATTER

Any first time visitor to Lourdes will not fail to notice the large number of uniforms to be encountered in the streets. People wearing a wide variety of insignia of many Orders are usually the nursing and other staff coming with a Pilgrimage group to look after the sick people they have brought with them.

There are two hospitals which are maintained to cater for these sick pilgrims. Notre Dame is within the Domaine, the other – St Frai – is just outside but close enough to wheel the patients in their chairs to the Grotto or the baths. Each Pilgrimage comes as a self contained unit, with its own doctors and nursing staff plus the required number of helpers.

The **Order of the Hospitalite** is a body of voluntary workers, with an office in the Domaine. They go through a period of training, and then must commit themselves to give a minimum number of days each year to their duties. The men are caled **"Brancardiers"**, the women **"Handmaids"**, or Nurses, and they wear a special badge on a pale blue ribbon with an inverted cross. Their duties will range from helping to unload sick people from the trains at the railway station, to stewarding at the processions and large masses, acting as hospital porters, bath attendants and laundry workers.

Lourdes comes with the Diocese of Lourdes and Tarbes, and the Bishop is in overall charge. The Rector of the Sanctuaries takes on the spot responsibility and he is helped, especially in programming the Masses, by the General Secretary.

Each of the sanctuaries is under the charge of a Chaplain, and there are also chaplains taking charge of Music, of the Grotto, of the Press, the grounds and so forth. Superiors of the Order of the Sisters of Charity of Nevers – to which Bernadette belonged – are in charge of each of the Hospitals, and the total staff based permanently in Lourdes is over 200 to cope with the annual influx of around five million pilgrims

Part 6
EXCURSIONS FROM LOURDES

LOURDES TO THE CIRQUE DE GAVARNIE
and the Pont D'Espagne

One of the most popular excursions from Lourdes will be that to the **CIRQUE de GAVARNIE** which has been described as one of the most spectacular sights in Europe. 'Cirque' in this context, means amphitheatre – a great wall of mountains surrounding a plain, some 9000m wide and the mountain 'wall' is about 1,400m high.

To get there take the road southwards via the spa town of Argelès-Gazost, with good views of the Pibeste mountain (1,349m). There is a turn-off here which can be used for a separate trip to the Ossau and Aspe Valleys. A little further on is the attractive village of **Saint-Savin** with half timbered houses and a fortified Abbey church. This was once a centre for the Cagot people (see below) and the Abbey has a low window designed to enable them to watch the services from outside the building. It also has an organ with grotesquely carved heads and faces which moved when the instrument was played. The village is just off the main road and provides good views – a worthwhile diversion.

Off the other side of the main road is a 12th century ruined Chateau at Beaucens where birds of prey are kept and displayed. It is known as Donjon des Aigles. Displays are given each afternoon in the season. The next town, Pierrefitte-Nestalas is remarkable only for a chemical factory, but there is a worthwhile diversion here to the Spa town of **CAUTERETS**, 30Km from Lourdes. The town was patronised by such as Georges Sand, Victor Hugo and Alfred Lord Tennyson. It offers cures for rheumatism and respiratory complaints but is now better known as a centre for winter sports. Some 6Km further along this road is the **PONT D'ESPAGNE**; a scenic old bridge and a series of waterfalls make attractive viewing. In French literary circles it is known as the place where Chateaubriand finally met Léontine de Villeneuve.

Returning to our original route, we come to another spa town in **LUZ ST SAVEUR** at the confluence of the Pau and Baston rivers. This also has a fortified church, founded by the Knights of St John of Jerusalem. Napoleon III caused the building of the Pont Napoleon in 1860 and the Chapelle Solférino.

Several new winter sports resorts have been built in this area in recent years to serve the slopes of the Pic du Midi de Bigorre, giving a year-round income from tourism.

And so we come to **GAVARNIE**, but not before stopping just above Gédre, from which there is a splendid view of the **BRÈCHE de ROLAND** – a 100m x 40m 'gateway' in the wall at the top of the Cirque, and the zenith of attainment for walkers in this area.

The village of Gavarnie, which is at 1,360m, is there mainly to serve the coachloads of tourists with the usual trappings of souvenir shops and cafes, but it has a proud history of mountaineering and exploration. It calls itself the 'Chamonix of the Pyrenees' and in particular has a statue of Count Henry Russell, an eccentric climber and explorer who pioneered the exploration of the area and especially loved the highest peak in the area, the Vignemale (3,298m). Russell carved out a number of caves on the mountains, and lived in them, sometimes throwing huge parties, but at other times doing the full social round of the season in Pau. He lived from 1834 to 1909, a Frenchman with an Irish father. It is a reminder that the major exploration of the Pyrenees was taking place during the lifetime of Bernadette Soubirous.

The **CIRQUE DE GAVARNIE** is an hour's walk from the village, or you can take one of the several hundred horses and mules on offer. You will pass the Grande Cascade, source of the Gave de Pau, which falls some 423m, and have fine views of the ridge of the Cirque, which forms the border with Spain. If you want to climb up to the Brèche du Roland, be prepared for a four hour stiff walk, but you will be rewarded with spectacular views into the Ordesa Canyon with 1,000m high walls.

The other major peak in this area is Mt Perdido (3,298m) on the Spanish side, and the centre of the Ordesa National Park which is the Spanish equivalent to the National Park of the Pyrenees in which we now are. There are other Cirques too, though none are quite as spectacular as the Gavarnie; the Cirque de Troumouse, broader than Gavarnie, and Estaube, both remote and accessible mainly to hikers, though there is a toll road part way to Troumouse.

THE NATIONAL PARK OF THE PYRENEES

A broad band that follows the line of the mountains for some 60 miles, the National Park – and its neighbouring Spanish counterpart, the Parque Nacional de Ordesa, are an attempt to preserve what is best in the natural habitat of so much wildlife. The main entrance is along the valley of the Pau from Lourdes to Gavarnie and you may be rewarded with a sighting of numerous birds of prey, some of them quite rare, such as the griffon vultures or the even rarer lammargeier or bearded vulture. Golden eagles might be visible, and also plenty of kites. The very rare Pyrenean brown bear is most unlikely to make an appearance – there are thought to be only a handful left – but you may well see ibex and in some places the mouflon – a large sheep with black horns which exists here and also in Cyprus and one or two other places. More common are izards (or chamois), a relative of the antelope, and there are many deer in the forested areas. In summer, there are exotic types of butterflies and you are likely to come across salamanders and many other kinds of lizard.

Wild flowers are very plentiful, with many of the rare species protected. More than 400 indigenous species include several types found only in the Pyrenees and the keen plant hunter will need to buy a book that illustrates them. For those who just like to see and enjoy, there is a veritable paradise of colour, especially in spring, with wild daffodils, blue gentians, a few orchids, lily and fritillary, and the heathers covering the slopes throughout the summer.

Remember though, that the obvious rules of any natural area apply also here and do nothing which will damage the environment for those who come after you. Dogs are not allowed in the park, neither is camping or caravanning, except bivouacking by genuine hikers, for whom there are several refuges offering basic accommodation.

If you take the excursions from Lourdes to Gavarnie and (especially) the Pont d'Espagne, you should get a good flavour of the park.

COASTAL AQUITAINE and the Pays Basque

It is about 100 miles or 150Km from Lourdes to the coast, but there is access by rail and excursions by coach are sold. If you are driving, most of the journey can be done by the Autoroute A64, on which tolls are payable. It makes for a long day, but a worthwhile one, and if you can stop over a night or two and

THE CAGOTS

A strange and remote people, the Cagots have a misty history. They lived in the middle ages and possibly had a form of leprosy though it doesn't seem to have been catching. They inhabited the Pyrenees region in both Spain and France. Treated as outcasts, they were denied social and political rights. They lived in ghettos in such towns as St Savin, Cauterets and St Jean Pied de Port, and wore a distinctive costume which included a piece of red cloth in the shape of a duck's or goose's foot. They were not allowed to mix with those outside their own but could trade with and observe the outside world from close quarters. Many churches had low windows, through which they could watch the services in progress, and they developed skills in carpentry and other trades but had to keep social contact within their own communities. They seem to have gradually become absorbed into the general population.

Bayonne

continue into Spain, the rewards are still greater. The excursions may only visit Biarritz, which is a pity since both Bayonne and St Jean de Luz are each worth a day at least.

It is best to start in **BAYONNE** which, though not strictly on the coast is virtually joined to the major resort of Biarritz.

Bayonne is the capital of the **BASQUE COUNTRY**, and we should perhaps start by looking a little at the history and culture of these highly independent people. Their origins are shrouded in some mystery, though it is certain that they go back a very long way. They have a language of their own- called Euskara, which though very much in a minority tongue spoken by about half a million Basques, gives them a sense of identity and can itself be traced back some 3,000 years. The Basques across the border in Spain have a violent recent history of rebellion in fighting the cause of independence and separation, but this is not a cause shared by the French Basques, who have not shown any desire to be united with their Spanish brethren. The Spanish independence movement, ETA has had no great support in France, especially since the death of Franco and the setting up of a Parliament for the Spanish Basques. Nonetheless, the French Pays Basque, and Bayonne in particular, acted as a haven for the Spanish Basques on the run from authority.

You will notice a difference in the architecture of the Pays Basque from that of the rest of the Pyrenees. The Basque village consists of stone built houses, white painted and with a reddish brown coloured half timbering, sometimes with overhanging upper stories or balconies, and with red pantile roofs.

A sure sign that you are in Basque country are the high walls of the Pelota Courts which feature in almost every village. This game, a very fast and dangerous version of squash, is an outward sign of the Basque male character, which is muscular and manly, and the area also contains some of the best French rugby teams and is home to several of their top stars in the sport.

Basque food and drink also has a character of its own, but we shall deal with that in a later chapter.

But to return to Bayonne. The town is dominated by the massive Citadel, built in 1680 as a defence against the Spaniards. During the Napoleonic wars, the French held out against Wellington, who put the town under siege for several months in 1813. The town stands at the confluence of the rivers Adour and Nive, and the old town spans both banks of the Nive, with a long bridge over the Adour connecting with the modern town, the station and the shopping centre. The old town and quays have a lot of character and the narrow streets are usually full of activity, especially on market days – Tuesday, Thursday and Saturday, which are a good time for a visit. The Musée Basque is sited in an old Basque town house on the Quai des Corsairs and reflects Basque

Statue of Our Lady, Biarritz

life and history and has a good maritime section – the Basques have a long association with the sea and with exploration. The other Museum, the Bonnat, has an impressive art collection given by the portrait painter Léon Bonnat, who died in 1922. It contains works by Goya, El Greco and Rubens. The Cathedral, on the opposite side of the Nive, dates from around 1260 with a gloomy Gothic interior offset by some rather good stained glass. The 13th century cloister – one of the largest in France – and enclosed gardens are worth a look.

BIARRITZ is the archetypal resort of the rich and famous. In the high summer, it may be worth spending a small fortune on a drink or a coffee to watch the parade of the smart set along the sea front. Its heyday was in the 19th century when it was a favourite watering place of the Empress Eugenie, wife of Napoleon III. The town has some excellent beaches, is a great centre for surfing, and has some excellent, but expensive, sea food restaurants. There is little of historical value, save for a watch tower which reminds one that this was once a whaling port. The best views are obtained from the lighthouse on the P'te St Martin, but look also for the statue of Our Lady on the R'er de la Vierge, close to the centre of the seafront.

ST JEAN de LUZ is an attractive town in an enclosed bay with excellent beaches, and a picturesque harbour which caters for both a fishing fleet and pleasure craft of every type. Some 15Km south of Biarritz, St Jean has a special place in the history of France as the place where the Sun King, Louis XIV

St Jean de Luz

married the Infanta of Spain, Maria Teresa, in June 1660. The wedding took place in the Church of St John the Baptist, which is the biggest and most beautiful of the Basque churches, with splendid three-tiered timber galleries. The Maison Louis XIV was the house where the King stayed prior to the marriage and is now open to visitors. Opposite is the Maison de l'Infante where Maria Teresa stayed, an Italianate style pink-washed house. All these are around the harbour, and in the same area is a number of smart restaurants – the town is a gastronomic centre with excellent seafood.

The neighbouring town of **CIBOURE** was the home of the composer Marcel Ravel and his Dutch style house on the harbour front can also be seen. All along the Basque Coast are beautiful sandy beaches, lovely bays and splendid views which make it a rival to the Cote D'Azur for the holiday spending of the French.

HENDAYE, the last town in France, stands on the River Bidassoa which marks the border with Spain. A tiny island in the river, the Ile des Faisans belongs equally to both nations and has traditionally been a meeting point for the heads of government, from the signing of the Treaty of the Pyrenees in 1659 and the signature of the marriage contract between Louis XIV and Maria Teresa a year later. The bridge which crosses the river – and the border – has seen traffic of every form over the centuries. Many Allied servicemen were smuggled into Spain this way – and over the mountain tracks nearby, during World War II and since then the Basque separatist leaders used the same route to escape in the opposite direction.

The first Spanish town you will come to is **FUNTERRABIA** – an atmospheric, walled and fortified town reminding you that it is also a border post and has seen many wars between the two countries. It is dedicated to Our Lady of Guadaloupe, who is claimed to have saved the town from a French siege in 1638 and is honoured by a great fiesta in early September. The wooden beamed houses remind you also that you are still in the country of the Basques, but wrought iron balconies, heavily studded doors and the many coats of arms displayed, make this a most attractive town to wander through.

There is a Gothic, mainly 16th century church and above the town, the Palace of Charles V, which dates from the 10th century is now one of the most famous Paradors, the state owned hotel chain renowned for the quality of their restaurants.

We shall proceed on this journey just another 23Km to the city of **SAN SEBASTIAN**. A city of 183,000 inhabitants, and one of Spain's largest, it serves as regional Capital, and is a centre of industry, as well as being a resort with excellent beaches and an attractive Old Town.

The Old Town was, in fact, almost totally re-built after a fire in 1813 – caused by British and Portuguese troops celebrating victory over the French – but in a manner which has preserved its character. The wide boulevard known as the Alameda marks the dividing line between old and new, and this is where the

Funterrabia

evening stroll takes place, leading up to the Plaza de la Constitucion and the Paseo. Bullfights used to take place in the Plaza, viewed from the balconied houses around it. The Museo de San Telmo, housed in a 16th century former Convent, will give you a Spanish version of Basque history, but also has a good collection of paintings, by El Greco and Goya. The Church of Santa Maria by the harbour is 18th century but has an elaborate Basque facade. There is also the 16th century Gothic Church of San Vicente, which has much earlier foundations.

San Sebastian

The sandy La Concha bay with its promenade is framed to the north by the bulk of Monte Urgull, topped by a huge statue of Christ and you can walk up to it by paths through the park. Superb views can also be obtained if you climb Monte Igueldo, at the southern end of the bay, accessible by funicular.

San Sebastian is a city of broad avenues, elegant buildings, and elaborate monuments. It is also a city of picturesque narrow streets around the harbour, of excellent restaurants, of fiestas, fishing and finery. Don't miss it if you can help it.

Heading west of San Sebastian on the A8, or on the N-634 if you want to hug the coast, then turning south along the Urola River, it is a short distance to the town of Azpeitia and neighbouring **LOYOLA**. The brithplace of St. Ignatius of Loyola, the founder of the Society of Jesus (the Jesuit order) is dominated by the fine Basilica by Carlo Fontani, a student of Bernini. The many highlights include the ornately carved stone covering the dome, and the silver clad statue of the Saint at the Altar. Ignatius'house is now a museum telling his story and the founding of the Order, and among the rooms of the house is a chapel for quiet prayer. The ancient town is dominated by the massif of Izarraitz – all in all a very pleasant part of the Basque countryside.

Basilica of St Ignatius of Loyola

THE PILGRIMAGE ROUTE OF ST JAMES
and the Western Pyrenees

Whilst still in the Basque country, we may explore a different way back to Lourdes from the coast which avoids the main roads, and follows the attractive valley of the Nive. This road (D932/918) follows the river from Bayonne and passes through the town of **Cambo les Bains**, a typical Basque community and the birth place of Edmond Rostard, who wrote Cyrano de Bergerac. His house is now a museum.

But this tour will also make a separate outing of great value as a day trip from Lourdes, or longer if you can cross into Spain. You can use the motorway A64 as far as the turn-off to Salies de Béarn and Sauveterre – both attractive towns worth a stop.

The body and head of the Apostle James are said to have been interred at the Spanish city of Santiago de Compostella, a city which became one of the earliest of Christian Pilgrimage centres, which it remains to this day. There is, to be frank, no real evidence whatever to suggest that St James was ever in Spain or that his remains could have been brought there, but tradition is

The Way of St James

what matters, and Santiago has been the object of veneration from the 9th century onwards. Four pilgrim routes through France became well established, and three of them starting from Paris, Le Puy and Vézelay, all converge near St Jean Pied de Port and cross the Spanish border to Roncesvalles. The fourth route, which started from Arles, crosses the Pyrenees further east and all link up south of Pamplona for the journey across northern Spain, which is marked by some magnificent romanesque architecture in the Cathedrals of towns such as Burgos, Léon and Lugo. But that is for another Pilgrimage, another book ...!

The route from Le Puy, itself a great religious centre, has been designated a national footpath or Grande Randonnée, and known as the GR65, or Chemin St Jacques, it is well marked throughout, the scallop shell insignia of St James being often spotted. It is a journey of around 800Km from Le Puy to Roncesvalles on the Spanish side of the border, and then another 790Km to Santiago itself. Those who complete the Pilgrimage route on foot today well deserve their certificate, or compostella, they get at the end.

The three routes converge near **St Palais**, where there is a museum dedicated to the pilgrimage route, and follows the general route of the D 933 towards St Jean Pied de Port. At **Ostabat** is the Maison Ospitalia, a cross between hospital and hostel, which in the middle ages would accommodate up to 5,000 pilgrims at a time. **St Jean Pied de Port** (the name means 'foot of the pass') was the last resting place before the 10Km climb to the Spanish border and the Ibaneta Pass. It is a lovely little town, well worth a visit, standing astride the River Nive. You enter by the Porte de St Jacques and depart by the Porte d'Espagne, but in between will want to see the massive Citadel built in 1688. Now a college, the view from the top is spectacular, which makes the steep climb worthwhile. The Vieux Pont which spans the river is highly photogenic, with old balconied houses bedecked with flower baskets, and leads to the Porte Notre Dame and the gothic, rather plain, 14th century church of that name. The town was formerly Spanish, which is reflected in the architecture, and only became French following the Treaty of the Pyrenees in 1659. The other building of interest is the old Bishops prison (des Evèques) at the top of the hill, which is now a museum. St Jean is a Basque town, though that is hardly reflected in its architecture, but it is a great centre of Pelota. If you have time for a meal, you should try the locally caught trout from the Nive.

The road to the border is also known as the Route Napoleon and he crossed this way, firstly to conquer, but then in retreat, being chased by Wellington after the Peninsular War. The route was also taken by the Black Prince to the Battle of Navarrate (1367). If you have time to cross into Spain, about 7Km from the border you will come to **Roncesvalles**, (Roncevaux in French), the first and major stop in Spain for pilgrims to Santiago. It is at the Abbey here that serious pilgrims receive from the Abbot their 'itinerario', a kind of passport which they can have stamped at the various stations en route to Santiago. The monastery was an Augustinian foundation dating

St Jean de Port

from about 1230. Somewhat disappointing architecturally – a rather ramshackle appearance – its founder, Sancho the Strong of Navarra was one of the heroes of the defeat of the Moors in 1212. His tomb is topped by an effigy of the man, said to be life size, in which case he was well over 7ft tall. The church is French gothic, built on top of Spanish Romanesque, reflecting the turbulent history of the area. There is a Treasury containing much memorabilia of pilgrimages past, and a fine gothic cloister which was rebuilt after a fire in 1400.

You will have travelled down to Roncesvalles via the **Ibaneta Pass**, which is the traditional site of the destruction of Charlemagne's army, ambushed by Basques in revenge for his sacking of Pamplona in 778. One of Charlemagne's knights, Roland, who commanded the rearguard and was killed in the battle, was the subject of the legendary **Chanson de Roland** or song of Roland, a lengthy epic ballad depicting the battle. His bravery was held as an example to armies throughout Europe before commencing battles and he is well commemorated in this area, as at the Brèche de Roland on the Cirque de Gavarnie.

It will be a drive of around 40Km further to **Pamplona** (see page 50) but if you are able to stay at least one night in Spain, the extra miles will be well justified. Pamplona is the capital of the province of Navarra – once a Kingdom – and is best known to tourists as the scene of the famous Bull Running, through the streets at the festival of San Fermin. It starts from the Bull Ring at the Plaza de Toros and the festival lasts for a week in early July with bull fights the other main attraction. If you are not addicted to this kind of 'sport' the place is best avoided at that time, for it will certainly be crowded. However, Pamplona has much else to detain you. The architecture ranges from the classically styled Parliament of Navarra, via the unusual porticoed and fortified Church of St Nicholas to the 18th century facade of the Cathedral, which replaced the original 14th century romanesque. The Cathedral contains the tombs of King Carlos III and his Queen Leonor carved in alabaster, and there is a fine 14th century Chapel of Barbazan and other finely sculpted stonework. Every good Spanish city has a Paseo, for the evening stroll, which in this case leads up to the Citadel, which has unusually low walls and was built to a star shaped pattern by Felipe II. The Citadel these days contains a series of exhibition halls and is surrounded by a pleasant park. There are several other churches worth a look; the Museum of Navarra, housed in a former hospital has some excellent paintings, including three Goyas, as well as exhibits from pre-history, Roman, medieval and contemporary periods, including a collection of icons.

Pamplona may well detain you for more than a day, and you can complete a round trip back to Lourdes by taking the pass over the Col du Somport, bringing you through the main part of the National Park of the Pyrenees, close

Pamplona

by the Cirque de Lescun (but you will have to walk at least 6Km to see it), and then along the Valley of the Aspe to Oloron St Marie before you can complete a circuitous route back to Lourdes.

SIERRA DE ARALAR and SAN MIGUEL IN EXCELSIS

An excursion which can be done from Pamplona, or alternatively if you have time to make a circular tour via San Sebastian, is the limestone 'karst' massif of Aralar. These days popular with walkers, it is home to the 10th century Sanctuary of San Miguel in Excelsis. Exiting the A-15 at Arakil, follow the A-10 to Uharte-Arakil and then ascend the steep but well-maintained mountain road, or walk up following National Path GR20.

The legend of a banished knight who enlisted the help of the Archangel Michael to repel a dragon is venerated in a statue of St Michael, and a chapel inside the beautifully preserved Sanctuary. Other highlights include an enamelled byzantine 'retablo' by the Sanctuary's altar and the fine views of the mountain range.

Sanctuary of San Miguel in Excelcis

THE LAC D'ARTOUSTE and COL du POURTALET

This excursion offers an alpine experience, including a ride in a cable car and another on a mountain railway.

The route follows the Ossau Valley, via Louvie-Juzon and Laruns. From the little lakeside village of Fabrèges, visitors are taken by cable car to the Pic de Sagette, a 2,000 metre peak and then by train on a 10Km ride through magnificent alpine scenery with wild flowers and rhododendrons, and across the ski slopes to the top of the station from which there is a short walk to the Lake, one of the highest (1,989m) in the mountains. The cable cars take six people each and the ride takes about eight minutes. The train ride is about 50 minutes each way and you will have around an hour and a half at the top.

The excursion buses usually take you to the top of the Pourtalet Pass (1,800m) and the Spanish frontier before returning to Lourdes. If you haven't tried these modes of transport before in other mountainous countries, you may well find the experience rewarding, but you need a nice day.

BAGNÈRES DE BIGORRE

This is an elegant spa town, some 22Km from Lourdes, which like Pau was originally Roman but saw its Thermal Establishment revived in the 19th century with a large Brititsh community quickly following. Among them were explorers and climbers such as Charles Packe, Henry Russell and Maxwell Lyte, all revered names in the history of mountaineering. Bagnères today has a lot to entertain the visitor, including two excellent museums – the Musée Salies, with a good art collection, and the Musée du Vieux Moulin, a folk museum contained in an old mill by the River Adour. The Thermal Establishment specialises in the treatment of rheumatism.

Two Kilometres south of the town are the **GROTTES DE MÉDOUS**, one of the most impressive of the grottoes in the Pyrenees, especially the grand cavern known as the Orchid House. These caves were discovered only in 1948. Guided tours take you on a 45 minute visit, which ends with a boat ride. The route is about a kilometre long and there are some steps to negotiate. As with all grotto visits, take a coat.

Bagnères will feature in a day tour called the Route des Lacs, which will take you over the Col d'Aspin (1,489m) and through the Aure Valley, via the winter sports resort of St Lary Soulon to lakes and waterfalls under the massif de Néouvielle, much of which is now a nature reserve. From the turn-off at Fabian, instead of returning to St Lary and Arreau, you could, if you have independent transport, make the short journey into Spain by the Bielsa Tunnel which in the space of 3Km, or about 5 minutes, will bring you to a totally different climate and vegetation – the Spanish side is remote and barren, and you may have come from rain or mist to hot sun.

Adventurous motorists may like to return to Lourdes by the Col du Tourmalet, to Luz St Sauveur (see also the Gavarnie route). This will bring you alongside the Pic du Midi de Bigorre, at 2,865m one of the highest peaks in the region. There is an observatory and radio station at the top and you can drive almost to the peak by a toll road. There has been a lot of winter sports development in this area in recent years.

PAU

Pau (pronounced PO) is but a thirty minute rail journey from Lourdes – by road about 40Km – so it is well within the compass of any visitor and is well worth a day. If travelling by car, you could take the old road (D937-8) and visit the grottoes at Bétharram (see page 35) on the way.

From the railway station there is a free funicular which carries you up to the main part of the town, which stands on a plateau, though it is only 200m above sea level. You emerge from the funicular on the famous **BOULEVARD DES PYRENEES** which runs the length of the town and from which there are stupendous views looking south towards the mountains. It is said that on a clear day no less than 80 mountain peaks can be identified over a scan of some sixty miles. To help you do this, there is a Table d'Orientation just to the right of the funicular station, which is a good place to start. The French poet, Lamartine said that if Naples has the world's finest view to the sea, then 'Pau must have the most beautiful continental vision.'

There are two factors which make Pau especially attractive to the British visitor. One is the British influence, which started from around 1815 when a large number of officers of Wellington's army came here to retire and started a British colony which lasted until the Second World War. Though it is not a Spa, Pau has the general ambience of towns such as Bath or Harrogate with the added spice of a continental flavour. And it has the climate to suit, with a very small difference in temperature between winter and summer. The British influence is still evident in the number of Tea Rooms, the Casino, and the emphasis on the horse, for which Pau is well known and much visited – even by the French. With its flower filled, tree lined squares and promenades, Pau is a highly fashionable resort and shopping centre, and so a magnet for the tourist.

Pau is important also in French history as a centre of Royalty, which is the other affinity it has with the British. It is the birthplace of King Henri IV of France, one of the outstanding Monarchs in French history. He was the first Protestant King of France, a fact which arose from the religious wars of which Pau was a centre. But in order to assimilate Paris and the North into his kingdom, Henri became a Catholic, but insisted on the freedom of all Frenchmen to follow their own religious beliefs.

Pau was also the birthplace of the founder of the Swedish royal house of Bernadotte. The man who became King Charles XIV of Sweden in 1818, was one of Napoleon's generals and had a house in the town which is now a museum.

At either end of the Boulevard des Pyrenees are the **CHATEAU** and the Casino. The Chateau originates from the 12th century but was destroyed and replaced by a larger Chateau, which in turn was allowed to deteriorate until the major restoration was done for Louis-Philippe in the 19th century. Today it contains two museums. The **NATIONAL MUSEUM** has some furnished apartments, fine tapestries and memorabilia of Henri IV. On the third floor is the **MUSEE BÉARNAIS** a folk museum relating to that undefined region, the Béarn, of which Pau calls itself the capital. Béarn was a Viscountcy which stretched to the Spanish border – indeed the Viscounts of Béarn became also the Kings of Navarre in the 16th century.

The Museum most worth a look is the **MUSÉE DES BEAUX ARTS**, a gallery with a fine collection of paintings, spanning the centuries from the 14th to 20th and in which Rubens, El Greco and Degas are all represented, but there is also a collection by the only artist of note who really captured Pyrenean scenery, Eugène Déveris. Walk through the park by the Casino to reach it.

The town's other claim to fame is that it was here that the Wright Brothers made several early public flights and trained French pilots, and the aviation connection is maintained today with a Parachutists Museum.

There is a good tradition of cultural entertainment in Pau, with an annual festival, and son et lumiere performances at the chateau in summer (usually early July) on the royal history of the town. There is a modern University with a high reputation, and so a strong student population with its attendant wine bars and musical pubs, and there is horse racing and show jumping at the Hippodrome. If you are on a touring holiday, Pau would make a good centre to stay for a day or two.

A MOUNTAIN DRIVE

If you have your own transport and would like a highly scenic half day drive, this is a route for you to try. It's not for the faint hearted – the roads are often narrow and there are some sheer drops. Coaches and heavy transport cannot use the roads, so you will not have too much opposition and the roads are kept in good condition.

A Col is a mountain pass and the route will take you over two of them, the Col du Soulor, which is at 1,794m and the Col d'Aubisque, 1,709m. That's taking you to well over 5,500ft and you will feel as though you are really into the mountains. Needless to say, the scenery along practically the whole route is quite stunning and you will need to make several stops to appreciate it.

Leaving Lourdes for Argelés, you take the turn off there marked for Arrens and the Col du Soulor. If you are travelling early in the season there are notices posted at the foot of the roads telling you if the Cols are open, or still snowbound. Above Arrens there are lovely views down to the Monastery and along the Valley of the Arrens, across to the Pic du Midi d'Arrens and the Vignemale beyond it. At the summit there are refreshments, and you have an alternative shorter drive down to Ferrières, but it is a smaller road than the one which continues to the top of the Aubisque. You will also be missing out on some of the finest scenery to be found in the Pyrenees – the views on both sides are fantastic. You will see cows with bells round their necks, as in Switzerland, plus sheep, goats and horses roaming free. At the top of the passes you can often buy cheese direct from the farmers.

The descent is via the modern ski resort of **GOURETTE**, a highly unattractive place, which dies in the summer, but take a look inside the modern church which has some stained glass and a picture window to the mountains. Cable cars can take you from here high into the mountains. The other town on the descent is Eaux-Bonnes, another thermal station and an attractive little town, but a better stopping place is **LARUNS**, at the head of the Ossau Valley, where there is a choice of several cafes in the market square. Return to Lourdes by running off at Louvie-Juzon on the D35, for Bétharram.

Part 7
THE PRACTICALITIES

GETTING THERE

BY ROAD Driving to Lourdes means a journey of at least 650 miles from the Channel ports, depending on the route you choose, so you will need at least two days, preferably three. There are so many places to be seen en route that you may well need a longer holiday, just to arrive! But if you can bear to by-pass the Loire, the Dordogne and the wineries of the Bordeaux region, you will be rewarded with the possibility of exploring the Pyrenees, one of the less well beaten tourist tracks for the foreign visitor to France, and, we hope this book has shown, a very rewarding one to visit, with comparatively little traffic on the roads. There is no direct autoroute, but if you pick up the A10 at Tours join the A62 at Bordeaux and follow it as far as Agen and then travel via Auch and Tarbes, you will have as direct a route as any, but there are many alternative ways.

Many groups travel by coach and these usually take the motorways via Paris, Orleans, and Tours. On the A64 motorway, from Toulouse take exit 12 and coming from Bayonne it's exit 11 – then follow the N21. It's about a 24 hour journey, with regular stops en route and provides the most economical way of getting there. Some groups will make an overnight stop, Paris being the most popular.

Parking in Lourdes is not easy, neither is driving around the lower town around the Domaine because of the crush of the crowds, but there are 3,000 free parking places available. It would be as well, though, to ensure that your hotel has its own parking lot. (Car Hire, Driving in France – see A–Z)

BY AIR Whilst many Pilgrims will travel by charter flight into Lourdes/Tarbes Airport, which is between these two towns, at Ossun, about 10Km north of Lourdes on the N21, the onset of budget scheduled flights means the options have proliferated. Airlines, departure airports and timetables change from one season to the next, however, and Pilgrimages with wheelchair users will need to pay special attention to what airlines will allow, and charge. Pau-Pyrenees Airport plays an important role also in ferrying Pilgrims, while Toulouse-Blagnac airport, some 2 hours away, provides yet more options including routes shared between Air France and Delta among others.

BY RAIL A very large proportion of Pilgrims, including many from the UK, travel to Lourdes by train – usually by specially chartered trains which can accommodate several hundred people and travel non stop from the channel coast to Lourdes station – a journey of about 12 hours, usually overnight.

French Railways have many ambulance cars, specially adapted to carry sick people, and there are couchettes for the able-bodied. During the season, Lourdes has one of the busiest stations on the French rail network – it handles no less than 1% of all the passengers travelling by SNCF every year.

Regular rail services include the High Speed TGV – you can be there in six hours from Paris without changing trains. www.voyages-sncf.com

A view of the Domaine

FOOD AND DRINK

If you are driving south to the Pyrenees you will find plenty to distract you, not least the wine growing regions of the Bordeaux. There are ample opportunities to stop and visit, and to taste, in any of the major 'name' regions such as Médoc, which is between the Atlantic and the Gironde estuary, or Entre Deaux Mers, which is in fact between two rivers – the Garonne and Dordogne. With Bergerac to the east and Cognac to the north, there is plenty of choice, including Graves – around Bordeaux city, and smaller areas such as Barsac and Sauternes a little further south.

The southern wine growing areas such as Languedoc and Roussillon border the Mediterranean, well to the east of Lourdes, but the nearest Appellation Côntrollée area is Jurançon, which centres upon Pau. It produces sweet and medium dry white wines from the Manseng grape. There are also the country wines (vins de pays), many of which are very good, such as Cotes de Gascogne, but if you are going into Gascony you will hardly miss the aroma of Armagnac (the world's second greatest brandy), centres for which are Eauze, Condom and Auch. The same area is the home of Paté de Foie Gras, made from goose liver, and the Foie de Canard, from the liver of the duck.

Beer drinkers will not find a huge or satisfying choice. The beer is almost all of the light lager variety, mostly imported from Alsace. The cheapest way to drink is to ask for a 'demi pression' which will get you a third of a litre on draught. That's just under half a pint.

The food served to the vast majority of Pilgrims, in the 2 and 3 star hotels in Lourdes will be good, but plain by French standards and you may not get the flavour of the finest French cuisine. To do so, you must find a restaurant, of which there are plenty, both in the town (mainly in the upper town) and surroundings. The village of Adé, on the way to Tarbes, has several good restaurants which may not be cheap, but at least once in your stay you may be excused for pampering yourself.

Quite a number of restaurants regard themselves as specialists in fish dishes, and the large number of rivers in the area provide some of the finest fish you could want. Try the salmon from the Gave d'Oloron in the Béarn, or trout and char from the Aspe and Ossau further south. The river Nive, which runs through St Jean Pied de Port is famous for trout also, but of course you don't need to travel to find these delights – almost every restaurant will advertise them.

There is no special cuisine of the Pyrenean area, but look out for Poule au Pot, a chicken casserole dish invented by King Henri IV; the Onion Soup with garlic; and Garbure, a vegetable soup with added pork or goose. Dishes featuring rabbit or game will also be found. In the Basque areas, the meals will be more substantial, the meat fatty, and the cuisine takes on a rather rural look – pigs' trotters; something that resembles tripe; and the intestines of lambs are some of the ingredients often found.

There is a definite Spanish influence to the cooking, even outside the Pays Basque, in such things as Piperade, an omelette with tomatoes and pimentos, and with your morning coffee or afternoon tea, you might try the delicious Gateau Basque – a cake which is crisp on the outside but with a custard like soft centre.

For a quick snack or cheap meal, look for the notices in bars or cafes offering 'le snack' or casses-croute. These will provide omelettes, filled baguettes or croques-monsieurs, even a simple sandwich. Those establishments which describe themselves as Brasseries will serve either a full meal or a single course at any time of the day, whilst the restaurants tend to stick to the more formal hours of lunch and dinner. Many of them have fixed menus, with three course meals at a fixed price, but in all cases the price lists are displayed outside the premises. Watch out for service charge, which will be 15% on top of the prices shown unless the menu says it is 'service compris' (included). Either way, you don't need to tip as well.

For a take-away meal or picnic, look out for the Charcuterie, a glorified butcher's shop, which offers a vast variety of quiches, pies, cooked meats, salads and prepared meals. You can ask for a slice (tranche) or buy the whole thing, but the selection is usually mouth watering.

If you intend eating out regularly, and are not fluent in French, it is as well to take a dictionary which has a menu section, as you will rarely find an English translation available in restaurants. Whatever your choice – bon appetit, and 'a votre santé'!

AN A-Z DIRECTORY OF PRACTICAL INFORMATION

ACCOMMODATION No town in France has more hotel beds than Lourdes, except for Paris. The choice is therefore enormous and there is accommodation in every category from the Youth Camp, several camping and caravan sites, through to luxury hotels. Most pilgrims will stay in the two star hotels, though some will be in perfectly adequate one star ones. Rooms will be small but adequate, and certainly clean, and will normally have private shower and wc. Accommodation lists are available from the Tourist Office – see below.

CAR HIRE Hire cars can be picked up from Lourdes/Tarbes and Pau-Pyrenees airports and from Lourdes station. Companies include Europcar (www.europcar. com), Hertz (www.hertz.com) and Avis (www.avis.com). Some local car dealerships offer car hire if you arrive by other means and wish to rent a car for a day or two – look out for signs that say Auto-Occasions. (See also Driving, below)

CLIMATE and DRESS The summer weather can be very variable and change quickly. Be prepared for possible rain, but expect also some quite high temperatures – between 20C and 28C between May and September, or even higher, and with high humidity. Dress for summer but take a light waterproof and umbrella. Comfortable shoes are the other main essential – you will be doing a lot of standing and walking.

CONSULATE The nearest British Consulate is at 353 Boulevard du President Wilson 33073 Bordeaux Tel: 05-57-22-21-10 (http://ukinfrance.fco.gov.uk/en/)
The Irish Embassy is at 12 Avenue Foch 75116 Paris Tel: 01-44-17-67-00
The nearest USA Consulate is at 89 Quai des Chartrons 33300 Bordeaux Tel: 05-56-48-63-85
The Canadian Embassy is at 35, Avenue Montaigne 75008 Paris Tel: 01-44-43-29-00
Australia's Embassy is at 4 Rue Jean Rey Paris 75724 Tel: 01-40-59-33-00
New Zealand's Embassy is at 7ter, Rue Léonard de Vinci 75116 Paris Tel: 01-45-01-43-43
South Africa have their Embassy at 59, Quai d'Orsay 75343 Paris Tel: 01-53-59-23-23

CURRENCY The currency in France and in Spain is the Euro. Banks with exchange offices in Lourdes include: Credit Mutuel at 19 Place Marcadal; Societe General at 53 Rue de la Grotte; and Lourdes Change which has two Bureaux at 104 Rue de la Grotte and at 28 Avenue Bernadette Soubirous. ATM's are commonplace. The major credit and debit cards are widely accepted.

DRIVING Driving in France follows the normal international procedures, but beware of the 'Priorité a Droit' law, which means that traffic coming at you from a side road on your right has priority over you, unless you are on a main road which is so designated by the yellow diamond signs on your road. Remember also that you may not cross a solid white line in the centre of the road, unless there is also a broken line on your side of it.

ELECTRICAL The voltage is 200 – 220 and comes from round two pin sockets. UK and other overseas visitors will find they can operate shavers, hair dryers etc. with the normal continental adaptor.

EMERGENCIES The Emergency phone numbers are 15 for an Ambulance or 17 for the Police Rescue Service. From a mobile phone all emergency services are accessed by dialling 112. If you need a Doctor, the hotel will call one for you, or any pharmacy will supply addresses and phone numbers. British visitors are advised to take the European Health Insurance Card, obtainable from post offices or online, which gives equal rights to medical treatment under EU rules, but the procedure is complicated – you have to pay first and then obtain a refund – and you are well advised to take out travel insurance which includes Medical Expenses cover. Either way, make sure you obtain receipts for all expenditure so you can claim on your return home. Carry the policy with you and ensure it includes a 24 hour emergency repatriation service in case of serious illness or accident.

PASSPORTS and VISAS France is a member of the EU and so British and Irish visitors need just an ordinary Passport and no Visa is needed. Visas are not needed by nationals of Canada, the USA and Australia, but are required by those from many other countries, including South Africa. You should check on the latest position.

PUBLIC HOLIDAYS In France they are quite numerous and result in many services being unavailable. They include Easter Sunday and Monday, Ascension Day, Penetecost (seventh Sunday after Easter) and the following Monday; May 1st and May 8th (which is VE Day), July 14th (Bastille), August 15th (Assumption of the Virgin Mary), November 1st (All Saints Day), November 11th (Armistice), and Christmas and New Year's Days.

TOURIST INFORMATION There is an Information Office (known in France as the Syndicat d'Initiative) in the Place du Peyramale, in the upper town centre – telephone 62-42-77-40 If writing from abroad add the area, or zip code – 65100 Lourdes. E-mail info@lourdes-infotourisme.com.
In London the French Government Tourist Office is at 300 High Holborn London WC1V 7JH (http://uk.franceguide.com)
Visitors from the USA see http://us.franceguide.com
In Australia and New Zealand go to http://au.franceguide.com and in Canada there is the choice of English (ca-en) or French (ca), Japan (jp) etc.

WATER Yes, it is safe to drink, and should be, since it comes from the mountain springs, but it will be different in chemical make-up from what you are used to, it may not be advisable to consume it in great quantities. Perfectly all right for cleaning teeth or diluting whisky, but for table use, bottled mineral waters are safest. Ask for eau minerale; it comes with or without gas. Many people take the Lourdes Water from the taps near the Grotto back to the hotel for table use and this is quite acceptable. You can buy containers for it in any of the souvenir shops.

WEBSITES General websites that could prove useful in planning a trip:
www.france-voyages.com/en and www.france-for-visitors.com
For Midi-Pyrenees Region www.tourism-midi-pyrenees.co.uk
Lourdes' two principal sites for visitors are the Tourist Office
www.lourdes-infotourisme.com and the Domaine www.lourdes-france.org
www.wines-france.com is a useful introduction to France's wine regions
For visiting Spain http://wikitravel.org/en/San_Sebastian provides listings of sights, shops, cafes and hotels with a similar entry for Pamplona.
Those following part of The Way of St James may wish to make contact with the Society in their home country: The Irish Society is at www.stjamesirl.com
The British Confraternity of St James is at www.csj.org.uk and The American Association of Friends http://www.reocities.com/friends_usa_santiago

Part 8
A PROGRAMME FOR PRAYER

The essential message that the Blessed Virgin has brought to us in various appearances over the past two centuries or more, is for mankind to turn back to God (and to Christ – God made flesh) – in penance and faith.

So the devotions at Lourdes are intended to help each person to make that conversion to God by private and public prayer.

The daily public programme at Lourdes consists of divine adoration by:

a) attending Mass
b) participating in the Blessed Sacrament procession and Marian devotion at the
c) Torchlight Procession

These are the ceremonies that help us direct our hearts towards God. For our private devotions, we are asked to consider if our efforts at prayer will be assisted by:

a) meditating on the Blessed Sacrament (eg. by silent prayer, as in the Crypt)
b) meditating on the Way of the Cross
c) examining the symbolism of water in the Sacraments (eg. at the Grotto and Baths)

These personal efforts at conversion to God should come to fruition in the Sacrament of Reconciliation (eg. at the Chapel of Reconciliation), and at Holy Communion.

The Pilgrim's day will usually therefore begin with attendance at Mass. These are held in the Basilicas from 6AM until 11.30AM, at The Grotto between 6AM and 9.45AM, and the International Mass at the Basilica of St Pius X at 9.30AM on Wednesdays and Sundays, and on Feast days. Evening Masses start from 6PM. Notices are posted giving each day's programme with Masses in different languages at each location. Every Pilgrimage group will make its own arrangement as to the Mass its members will attend.

This may be followed by private prayer, possibly in the Crypt, or by making the Stations of the Cross, or possibly by bathing.

At the time of writing the Rosary is recited at the Grotto at 3.30PM

The Procession of the Blessed Sacrament commences at 5PM, starting from the Outdoor Altar on the Prairie and travelling around the Esplanade, and culminating in the Blessing of the Sick in the underground Basilica of St Pius X. If it is wet or extremely hot, the entire celebration takes place in the underground Basilica.

In the evening the great Torchlight Procession will start from the Prairie, commencing from 8.45PM; finishing with a service in Rosary Square. The last Mass of the day takes place at the Grotto, after the Procession at 11PM. Clearly not everyone will wish to follow all of this programme every day – indeed to do so would overstretch our spiritual and physical reserves of strength. There will be excursions and other visits to fit into the programme, but depending upon the length of your stay, you will want to fit in at least once:-

- Mass and Holy Communion
- The Sacrament of Reconciliation
- Visits for Private Prayer
- The Blessed Sacrament procession and Blessing of the Sick

DAY PILGRIMS' PROGRAMME

A special programme operates every day in July, August and September (enquire if visiting at other times of the year) for those who are on only a brief visit to Lourdes. It is possible to join an English speaking group under the leadership of a Priest. Assembly point is at 8.30AM by the Statue of the Crowned Virgin and the group is conducted to the Accueil Jean Paul II or across the river to the Prairie for prayers, followed by a welcome and explanation of the message of Lourdes.

At 9.30AM the Stations of the Cross are followed and at 11.15 attendance at Mass. In the afternoon, meet again at the Crowned Virgin Statue at 2.30PM for an explanatory visit to the places associated with Bernadette. At 5PM, join the Procession of the Blessed Sacrament, starting from the Prairie opposite the Grotto. There is then free time until 8.45PM, when Pilgrims may join the Torchlight Procession.

PRAYERS AND DEVOTIONS

We hope that the following prayers and devotions will help the reader to follow this programme, and may be useful in private prayer.

THE ROSARY

One of the devotions that is sometimes taken for granted is the recitation of the Holy Rosary. The Rosary does not feature prominently in the official programme of celebrations but, in a way, whenever a person is not engaged in other prayer, the Rosary should be on our lips (as it is when waiting at the Baths, as part of the Night Prayer at the Grotto, etc)

The Rosary is a prayer that focuses our mind on the more important moments of Our Lord's and Our Lady's lives (called the 'Mysteries' in this prayer). There are fifteen of them, dealing with Christ's early life (*Joyful Mysteries*), His Passion and Death (*Sorrowful Mysteries*), and the life of heaven (*Glorious Mysteries*).

The Joyful Mysteries
1. The Annunciation (The angel comes to Mary)   Luke 1.26-38
2. The Visitation (Mary visits Elizabeth)   Luke 1.39-56
3. The Birth of Jesus   Luke 2.1-20
4. The Presentation in the Temple   Luke 2.22-38
5. The Finding of the Child Jesus in the Temple   Luke 2.41-50

The Sorrowful Mysteries
1. Prayer and agony in the Garden   Luke 22.39-46
2. Scourging at the Pillar   Luke 23.16-17
3. Crowning with Thorns   Mat. 27.27-30
4. Carrying the Cross   Mat. 27.31-38
5. Crucifixion and Death   Mat. 27.35-38

The Glorious Mysteries
1. Resurrection   Mat. 28. 3-8
2. Ascension   Mark 16.19
3. Coming of the Holy Spirit on the Apostles   Acts 2.1-13
4. Assumption of Our Lady into heaven
5. Crowning of Our Lady and Glory of the Saints

The prayer is said by reciting for each Mystery (or decade)
     one Our Father
     ten Hail Marys
     one Glory be to the Father
concluding with the prayer Hail Holy Queen and the Rosary Prayer.

THE MASS

Since the Second Vatican Council the celebration of Mass has become less uniform, celebrants are encouraged to introduce variety into the choice of prayers, readings and music. So it is difficult to publish 'set piece' liturgies in a booklet such as this.

The Eucharistic prayers and Communion Rite may be found in a Sunday or Weekday Missal. The penitential rite and readings, homily and bidding prayers (Prayer of the Faithful) are mostly composed or chosen for each individual celebration.

In Lourdes, the authorities choose a theme for each year. That theme is used at the International Mass and Procession of the Blessed Sacrament. But as it changes each year it is not possible in this book to tell you what to expect it will be.

The best way of celebrating Mass in Lourdes is to be present in heart and mind to whatever is taking place in the action of the Mass, listening as carefully as possible in order to share as fully as one can in the prayer of that particular Mass community. It may help to have some idea of the structure of the Mass so that it may be possible to understand what is happening more quickly, especially if a foreign language is being used.

The Mass to be used after advent 2011 is composed of five sections.

1. The Introductory Rites
   - entrance Chant
   - greeting (eg. The grace of our Lord Jesus Christ etc.)
   - Pentiential Act (Have mercy on us, O Lord; or Kyrie eleison)
   - sometimes followed by a hymn (Glory to God in the highest etc.)
   - Silent prayer, followed by the Collect prayer

2. The Liturgy of the Word
   - readings, responsorial psalm
   - Alleluia (or other chant depending on liturgical calendar), incense (where used), Cleanse my heart and my lips etc.
   - reading
   - homily
   - creed and bidding prayers

3. The Liturgy of the Eucharist
   - preparation of the altar
   - bringing of the gifts (bread and wine)
   - offertory chant; Wash me O Lord etc.
   - 'Pray, brethren, that my sacrifice and yours may be acceptable to God, the almighty Father.'
     R/ 'May the Lord accept the sacrifice at your hands for the praise and glory of his name, for our good and the good of all his holy Church.'
     Prayer over the offerings.
   - Eucharistic prayer (one of four, some parts can be sung)

4. The Communion Rite
   - Our Father
   - sign of peace
   - 'Lamb of God, you take away the sins of the world, have mercy on us (2); grant us peace (1).'
   - 'May the receiving of your Body and Blood, Lord Jesus Christ, not bring me to judgement' etc.
   - Lord I am not worthy
   - distribution of communion
   - psalm or hymn may be sung
   - silent prayer; Prayer after Communion

5. The Concluding Rites
   - announcements
   - dismissal

PRAYERS

THE LORDS PRAYER
Our Father, who art in heaven, hallowed be Thy Name; Thy kingdom come; Thy will be done on earth as it is in heaven. Give us this day our daily bread; and forgive us our trespasses as we forgive those who trespass against us; and lead us not into temptation, but deliver us from evil.

Amen.

THE HAIL MARY
Hail Mary, full of grace! The Lord is with thee; blessed art thou amongst women, and blessed is the Fruit of thy womb, Jesus. Holy Mary, Mother of God, pray for us sinners, now and at the hour of our death.

Amen.

THE GLORIA
Glory be to the Father, and to the Son, and to the Holy Ghost; As it was in the beginning, is now, and ever shall be, world without end.

Amen.

THE MEMORARE
Remember, O most loving Virgin Mary,
that it is a thing unheard of
that anyone who ever had recourse to your protection,
implored your help and sought your intercession,
was left forsaken.
Filled, therefore, with confidence in your goodness,
I fly to you, O Mother, Virgin of virgins;
to you I come, before you I stand, a sorrowful sinner.
Despise not my words, O Mother of the Word,
but graciously hear and grant my prayer.

Amen.

HAIL HOLY QUEEN
Hail, holy Queen, mother of mercy; hail, our life, our sweetness, and our hope. To thee do we cry, poor banished children of Eve; to thee do we send up our sighs, mourning and weeping in this vale of tears. Turn then, most gracious advocate, thine eyes of mercy towards us; and after this our exile, show unto us the blessed fruit of thy womb, Jesus.
O clement, O loving, O sweet Virgin Mary.

ROSARY PRAYER
P: Pray for us, O holy Mother of God.
C: That we may be made worthy of the promises of Christ.
Let us pray.
O God, whose only-begotten Son, by His life, death and resurrection, has purchased for us the rewards of eternal life; grant, we beseech thee, that

meditating on these mysteries, in the most holy Rosary of the Blessed Virgin Mary, we may both imitate what they contain, and obtain what they promise, through the same Christ our Lord.

Amen.

ACT OF CONTRITION

O my God! I am heartily sorry for having offended You; I detest all my sins, not because I fear the pains of hell and the loss of heaven, but because they offend You my God, Who art all good and deserving of all my love. Lord! only with Your help can I avoid sin in the future, help me, dear Lord, to do Your Holy Will so that I may be found worthy to live for ever in Your love.

O God! the Creator and Redeemer of all the faithful, grant to the souls of Thy servants departed the remission of all their sins: that through pious supplications they may obtain that pardon which they have always desired: Who livest and reignest world without end.

Amen.

Come O Holy Spirit! Fill the hearts of the Faithful, and kindle in them the fire of Your divine love.

Our Father . . .   Hail Mary . . .   Glory be to the Father . . .

The Pilgrimage of Glasgow, Scotland

65

Part 9
THE WAY
OF THE CROSS

In Lourdes there are Stations of the Cross to be found on the hill directly across the road from the entrance to the Crypt of the Upper Basilica, at the far end of the Meadow (suitable for a person in a wheelchair) and around the processional way in the Basilica of St Pius X.

As in the Rosary we are presented with 15 incidents from the life of Jesus. This time from the last hours of his Passion and Death. On Good Friday the account of the Passion that is read is from St John's Gospel (chapters 18-20) so perhaps our prayer will be based on that reading which is probably familiar to us.

After the quotations from scripture St Alphonsus's suggestions for meditation are given. Our prayer will be to relate to Jesus's suffering for us as individuals and a world community.

1st Station

1st Station   JESUS IS CONDEMNED TO DEATH

John 19.5   Jesus came out wearing a crown of thorns and the purple robe. Pilate said 'Here is the man.' When they saw Him the chief priests and guards shouted 'Crucify Him, Crucify Him.' Pilate said 'Take him yourselves and crucify him: I can find no case against him.'

Consider how Jesus, after having been scourged and crowned with thorns, was unjustly condemned by Pilate to die on the cross.

2nd Station

2nd Station   JESUS RECEIVES THE CROSS

John 19.11   'You would have no power over me,' said Jesus, 'if it had not been given you from above.'

10.17   'The Father loves me because I lay down

my life in order to take it up again. No one takes it from me, I lay it down of my own free will.'

Consider how Jesus in making this journey with the cross on His shoulders, thought of us and offered for us to his Father the death He was about to undergo.

3rd Station	JESUS FALLS THE FIRST TIME
John 1.14	The word was made flesh, he lived among us.
1Cor 1.25	God's weakness is stronger than human strength.

Consider this first fall of Jesus under his cross. His flesh was torn by the scourges, his head was crowned with thorns, and he had lost a great quantity of blood. So weakened he could scarcely walk and yet he had to carry this great load upon his shoulders. The soldiers struck him rudely, and he fell several times.

4th Station	JESUS IS MET BY HIS MOTHER
Luke 2.34	Simeon blessed them and said to Mary, his mother, 'You see this child: he is destined for the fall and for the rising of many . . . and a sword will pierce your own soul too.'

Consider this meeting of the Son and the Mother which took place on this journey. Their looks become like so many arrows to wound those hearts which loved each other so tenderly.

5th Station	THE CROSS IS LAID UPON SIMON OF CYRENE
Mark 15.21	They enlisted a passer-by, Simon of Cyrene, father of Alexander and Rufus, who was coming in from the country, to carry his cross.

5th Station

Consider how the Jews, seeing that at each step Jesus was on the point of expiring, and fearing he would die on the way, whereas they wished him to die the shameful death of the cross, constrained Simon of Cyrene to carry the cross behind our Lord.

6th Station	VERONICA WIPES THE FACE OF JESUS
Mat. 26.36	'I was sick and you visited me, in prison and you came to see me.'

6th Station

26.40 'I tell you solemnly, insofar as you did this to one of the least of these brothers of mine, you did it to me.'

    Consider how the holy woman named Veronica, seeing Jesus so ill-used, and his face bathed in sweat and blood, wiped his face with a towel on which was left the impression of his holy countenance.

7th Station **JESUS FALLS THE SECOND TIME**

Mark 14.35 'My soul is sorrowful to the point of death ... he fell to the ground and prayed that, if it were possible, this hour might pass him by ... let it be as you, not I, would have it.'

    Consider this second fall of Jesus under the cross, a fall which renews the pain of all the wounds of his head and members.

7th Station

8th Station **THE WOMEN OF JERUSALEM MOURN FOR OUR LORD**

Luke 23.27 Large numbers of people followed him, and of women too, who mourned and lamented for him. But Jesus turned to them and said, 'Daughters of Jerusalem, do not weep for me, weep rather for yourselves and for your children. For the days will surely come when people will say "Happy are those who are barren, the wombs that have never borne, the breasts that have never suckled." Then they will begin to say to the mountains "Fall on us!' to the hills 'Cover us!' For if men use the green wood like this what will happen when it is dry?'

    Consider how those women wept with compassion at seeing Jesus in such a pitiable state, streaming with blood as he walked along.

9th Station **JESUS FALLS THE THIRD TIME**

Luke 22.56 As he was sitting there by the blaze, a servant girl saw him, peered at him and said, 'This person was with him too.' But he denied it. 'Woman,' he said, 'I do not know him.' Shortly afterwards someone else saw him and said, 'You are another of them.' But Peter replied, 'I am not, my friend.' About an hour later another man insisted, saying 'this fellow was certainly with him. Why, he is a Galilean.' 'My friend,' said

9th Station

Peter, 'I do not know what you are talking about.' At that instant . . . the cock crew . . . and Peter remembered.

Consider the third fall of Jesus Christ. His weakness was extreme, and the cruelty of his executioners excessive who tried to hasten his steps when he could scarcely move.

10th Station JESUS IS STRIPPED OF HIS GARMENTS

John 19.23 They took his clothing and divided it into four shares, one for each soldier. His undergarment was seamless, woven into one piece from neck to hem; so they said to one another, 'Instead of tearing it, let's throw dice to decide who is to have it.' In this way the words of the scripture were fulfilled:

They shared out my clothing among them   Ps. 22.18

10th Station

They cast lots for my clothes.

This is exactly what the soldiers did.

Consider the violence with which Jesus was stripped by the executioners. His inner garments adhered to his flesh, and they dragged them off so roughly that the skin came with them.

11th Station JESUS IS NAILED TO THE CROSS

Luke 23.33 When they came to the place called The Skull they crucified him there and the two criminals also, one on the right, the other on the left. Jesus said, 'Father forgive them; they do not know what they are doing.'

Consider how Jesus having been placed on the cross, extended his hands and offered to his eternal Father the sacrifice of his life for our salvation. Those barbarians fastened him with nails, and then securing the cross, allowed him to die with anguish on this infamous gibbet.

12th Station JESUS DIES ON THE CROSS

Luke 23.44 It was now about the sixth hour and, with the sun eclipsed, a darkness came over the whole land until the ninth hour. The veil of the Temple was torn right down the middle, and when Jesus had cried out in a

12th Station

loud voice, he said 'Father, into your hands I commit my spirit.'   (Ps 31.5)
With these words he breathed his last.

Consider how Jesus being consumed with anguish after three hours agony on the cross, abandoned himself to the weight of his body, bowed his head and died.

13th Station JESUS IS TAKEN DOWN FROM THE CROSS

Luke 23.51 Joseph of Arimathaea went to Pilate and asked for the body of Jesus. He took it down, wrapped it in a shroud and put him in a tomb which was hewn in stone in which no one had yet been laid. It was Preparation Day and the sabbath was imminent.

13th Station

Consider how after our Lord had expired, two of his disciples, Joseph and Nicodemus, took him down from the cross and placed him in the arms of his afflicted Mother, who received him with unutterable tenderness and pressed him to her bosom.

14th Station JESUS IS LAID IN THE SEPULCHRE

Luke 23.55 Meanwhile the women who had come from Galilee with Jesus were following behind. They took note of the tomb and of the position of the body. They then returned and prepared spices and ointments. And on the sabbath day they rested, as the Law required.

Consider how the disciples, accompanied by His holy Mother, carried the body of Jesus to bury it; they closed the tomb and all came sorrowfully away.

On the way down the hill from the main stations in Lourdes there is a 'fifteenth station'. 'The stone is rolled away from the tomb.' (Lk 24. 2-4) This is, of course, the first intimation of Christ's resurrection.

15th Station at ground level: Mary awaiting the Resurrection

70

THE LOURDES HYMNS

IMMACULATE MARY

Ave, Ave, Ave, Maria!
Ave, Ave, Ave, Maria!

Immaculate Mary!
Our hearts are on fire,
That title so wondrous,
Fills all our desire!

We pray for God's glory
May His kingdom come
We pray for his Vicar
Our Father, and Rome

We pray for our Mother,
The Church upon earth
And bless, sweetest Lady,
The land of our birth.

There is no need, Mary,
Nor ever hath been,
Which thou canst not succour,
Immaculate Queen.

O bless us, dear Lady,
With blessings from heaven,
And to our petitions
Let answer be given.

O Mary! O Mother!
Reign o'er us once more
Be England, thy dowry
As in days of yore

We pray for all sinners
And souls that now stray
From Jesus and Mary
In heresy's way

For poor, sick, afflicted,
Thy mercy we crave.
And comfort the dying,
Thou light of the grave.

In grief and temptation,
In joy, or in pain,
We'll seek thee, our Mother,
Nor seek thee in vain.

In death's solemn moment,
Our Mother, be nigh,
As children of Mary
O teach us to die.

HOLY VIRGIN

Holy Virgin, by God's decree,
You were called eternally,
That he could give his Son to our race,
Mary, we praise you: Hail, full of grace.

By your faith and loving accord,
As the handmaid of the Lord,
You undertook God's plan to embrace,
Mary, we thank you; Hail full of grace.

Joy of God you gave and expressed,
Of all women, none be more blessed,
When in mankind your Son took his place,
Mary, we love you; Hail full of grace.

Refuge for your children so weak,
sure protection all can seek;
Problems of life you help us to face,
Mary, we trust you: Hail, full of grace.

To our needy world of today,
Love and beauty you portray,
Showing the path to Christ we must trace,
Mary, our Mother: Hail, full of grace.